PROMISES & BLESSINGS

in the Book of Revelation

Doug Rowston

PROMISES & BLESSINGS in the Book of Revelation takes the reader on an interesting journey through the last book of the Bible. This study looks at seven promises to those who conquer the powers of evil and death by faith in Christ the Victor. It also looks at seven blessings for those who read, mark, learn and inwardly digest the message of the Revelation to John. A special feature is the inclusion of pen portraits of the Martyrs of the Twentieth Century whose statues adorn the west front of Westminster Abbey in London, England.

Rowston, Doug
PROMISES & BLESSINGS in the Book of Revelation

Published by
Grace & Peace Books
4A Wurilba Ave Hawthorn SA 5062 Australia
djrowston@gmail.com

© Douglas James Rowston 2014

This work is copyright. All photographs were taken by the author. Other than for the purposes and subject to the conditions prescribed under the Copyright Act, no part of it may in any form or by any means (electronic, mechanical, microcopying, photocopying, recording or otherwise) be reproduced, stored in a retrieval system or transmitted without prior written permission from the publisher.

First published 2015 by Morning Star Publishing
This edition published in 2022

ISBN 978-0-6453288-4-4

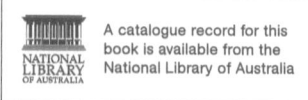

*This book is dedicated to
Basil S. Brown
and
William E. Hull
my mentors
in the study of the New Testament*

Acknowledgements

The Scripture quotations are from The New Revised Standard Version Bible, copyright © 1989, 1995 by the Division of Christian Education of the National Council of Churches of Christ in the U. S. A. Used by permission. All rights reserved.

Cover Photographs
Front: Cave of the Apocalypse   Patmos
Back: John the Theologian   Patmos

Contents

Preface		1
The Revelation to John in the First Century		3
Christian Martyrs of the Twentieth Century		11

PROMISES　　　　　　　　　　　　13

1	The Tree of Life	15
2	The Crown of Life	21
3	The Bread of Heaven	27
4	The Victory of God	33
5	The Book of Life	39
6	The Temple of God	45
7	The Throne of God	50

BLESSINGS　　　　　　　　　　　　55

8	The Reader and the Hearers	57
9	The Faithful Dead	62
10	The Sentinel	67
11	The Guests	73
12	The Holy and Hopeful	80
13	The Obedient	87
14	The Cleansed	91

PERPLEXING QUESTIONS & INTRIGUING ANSWERS   *95*

Who are the angels of the seven churches?   97
What does the book say about God and Jesus?   98
What sort of God do Christians believe in?   99
What did John expect to happen soon?   101
Who is past, present and future in the book?   102

Postscript   103

Appendix: Outline of the Book of Revelation   106
Select Bibliography   108

Christian Martyrs of the Twentieth Century

Grand Duchess Elizabeth	20
Manche Masemola	26
Maximilian Kolbe	32
Lucian Tapiedi	38
Dietrich Bonhoeffer	44
Esther John	61
Martin Luther King	66
Wang Zhiming	72
Janani Luwum	79
Oscar Romero	86

Preface

The book of Revelation continues to attract readers with its intriguing symbols and dramatic contents. George Beasley-Murray, James Blevins, George Caird, Colin Hemer and Stephen Smalley are among modern New Testament scholars who have written helpful commentaries. The present work focuses on the letters to the seven churches in chapters 2 and 3 as well as the seven blessings scattered throughout the rest of the book.

On the one hand, some parts of Revelation are more accessible to us. The letters to the seven churches have a regular pattern. Accordingly, we examine each letter with reference to the context, the description of Christ, the commendation and criticism of the church, the promise to the conqueror and some connections with today. On the other hand, other parts of Revelation can be hard to follow. Scattered through the book are seven blessings. By examining their contexts, contents and connections we may gain an appreciation of these 'beatitudes' and their contribution to the overall structure of this dramatic and intriguing concluding book of the Bible.

In addition, there are pen portraits of the ten martyrs of the twentieth century whose statues adorn the west front of Westminster Abbey. I was strangely moved when my wife and I visited London and saw the ten statues of such a varied group of Christians who died for their faith. The message of the Revelation to John addressed people who were willing to die as martyrs in the first century. The martyrs of the twentieth century who are remembered at Westminster Abbey represent countless Christians who have died in modern times for their faith in the Crucified and Risen Lord. The book of Revelation continues to speak to situations of persecution and oppression.

The exegetical insights and devotional reflections have been written for people both inside and outside churches. *Promises and Blessings* could well be of interest in home groups as well as for personal reading. The Revelation to John has an abiding relevance. John's expectation of the future, faith in God and patient waiting for divine action are features which spoke to past generations and continue to speak to us today.

The dedication indicates my indebtedness to Rev Dr Basil S. Brown, whose meticulous teaching encouraged my love of New Testament Greek at Whitley College in Melbourne, Victoria, and Rev Dr William E. Hull, whose inspired supervision made my doctoral studies at the Southern Baptist Theological Seminary in Louisville, Kentucky, so fulfilling.

I wish to thank my wife Rosalie for her patience and love during the writing of this book. I am also grateful to my brother Laurie for his conscientious checking of the completed draft of this work.

After working as a theological lecturer, a religious education teacher and a local church pastor, I was blessed in semi retirement to be adjunct lecturer at St Barnabas College in Adelaide, South Australia, in association with Charles Sturt University. I continued to learn with its faculty, staff and students of the grace and peace of Christ.

Doug Rowston

The Revelation to John in the First Century

A memorable statement about the Revelation (or Apocalypse) to John has been attributed to Martin Luther, the sixteenth century Protestant Reformer. He is supposed to have said, 'It may have been a revelation to John, but it is surely a mystery to me!' I say 'attributed to' because the saying is probably apocryphal. However, if we are to understand seven promises and seven blessings in the book, we need to consider its actual context, secret codes, literary category and thematic content.

Context of Revelation

Including martyrs ancient and modern, the book of Revelation gives promises and blessings to the followers of Jesus, the one who died and rose again. It is written by a prophet named John on the Isle of Patmos towards the end of the reign of Domitian in AD 96. It is directed towards believers in the western area of Asia Minor.

Dio Cassius, the Roman historian, says that Domitian moved against 'atheists' in AD 95. Because the Christians denied the reality of the traditional Roman gods, they were accused of atheism. Eusebius, the Christian historian, writes that Domitian 'with his hatred of God and his hostility to him . . . proved himself the successor of Nero'.

Nero had represented himself on coins as Apollo, god of the sun and son of Jupiter. Domitian goes further by issuing edicts with the words, 'Our Lord and God commands', and by requiring from his citizens the following greeting, 'Hail to the Lord of Lords!'

Codes of Revelation

The writer of the book of Revelation is a prisoner in a concentration camp on Patmos in the Aegean Sea about eighty kilometres (fifty miles) from Ephesus. He writes his book in a secret code to avoid incurring further punishment. The book is then passed around the seven churches on the mainland. He writes to encourage Christians in the face of severe persecution. His secret code is threefold: a number code, a colour code and an animal code.

Number Code	Colour Code	Animal Code
Fractions = Incompleteness	Pale Green = Death	Frog = Vileness
1 = Unity	Dark Green = Life	Eagle = Bad News
2 = Witnesses	White = Purity	Beast = Evil
4 = Corners of the Earth	Red = War	Beast from the Sea = Caesar
5 = Penalty	Black = Famine	Sea Serpent = Satan
6 = Imperfection	Gold = Worth	Locusts = Decadence
7 = Divine Number	Bronze = Strength	Lamb = Jesus
10 = Complete Number	Scarlet = Sin	Lion = Wild Creature
12 = Wholeness		Ox = Domesticated Creature

Neither the guards on Patmos nor the Romans in Ephesus understand these codes. When John sends his book to be read aloud in the seven churches, his fellow believers understand the secret codes but their persecutors do not. Consequently, the Christians receive his messages of hope in the midst of suffering. And they do so in safety. After all, some of his secret codes are quite unflattering to the emperor and to the practice of emperor worship.

Category of Revelation

The introduction of the book calls it a revelation (Latin) or an apocalypse (Greek): *The revelation of Jesus Christ (Revelation 1:1)*. With their number, colour and animal codes, revelatory or apocalyptic literature can be likened to political and religious cartoons.

The introduction of the book also calls it a prophecy: *Blessed is the one who reads aloud the words of the prophecy (Revelation 1:3)*. Prophecy is a forthtelling of God's judgement and mercy.

Finally, the introduction of the book implies that it includes letters or epistles: *John to the seven churches that are in Asia (Revelation 1:4)*. The letters are written for publication among the seven churches of the Roman province of Asia.

Content of Revelation

Like the composer of a symphony, John reworks his themes again and again. By so doing, John emphasises the final victory of God, God's Lamb and God's people over the powers of evil and death.

After the introduction of his revelation, prophecy and letters (Revelation 1:1-8), John portrays a vision of Christ who is the Son of Man promised in the Old Testament book of Daniel (Revelation 1:9-20).

Then he transmits letters to seven lampstands or churches in Asia Minor (Revelation 2:1 to 3:22).

Lampstands
Ephesus
Smyrna
Pergamum
Thyatira
Sardis
Philadelphia
Laodicea

Next John tells of a vision of the control room at the heavenly headquarters (Revelation 4:1 to 5:14). Every creature in the universe from the beginning of God's creation through all time to the end of God's creation sings praises to God the Creator and God the Redeemer. The readers of and listeners to the drama, which is the book of Revelation, are invited to join in the worship of the heavenly throng despite the earthly confusion surrounding them.

In the body of the book, John makes his readers stand back to absorb a general impression of God's judgement by means of seals (Revelation 6:1-17; 8:1-5), trumpets (Revelation 8:6 to 9:21; 11:15-19) and bowls (Revelation 15:1 to 16:21).

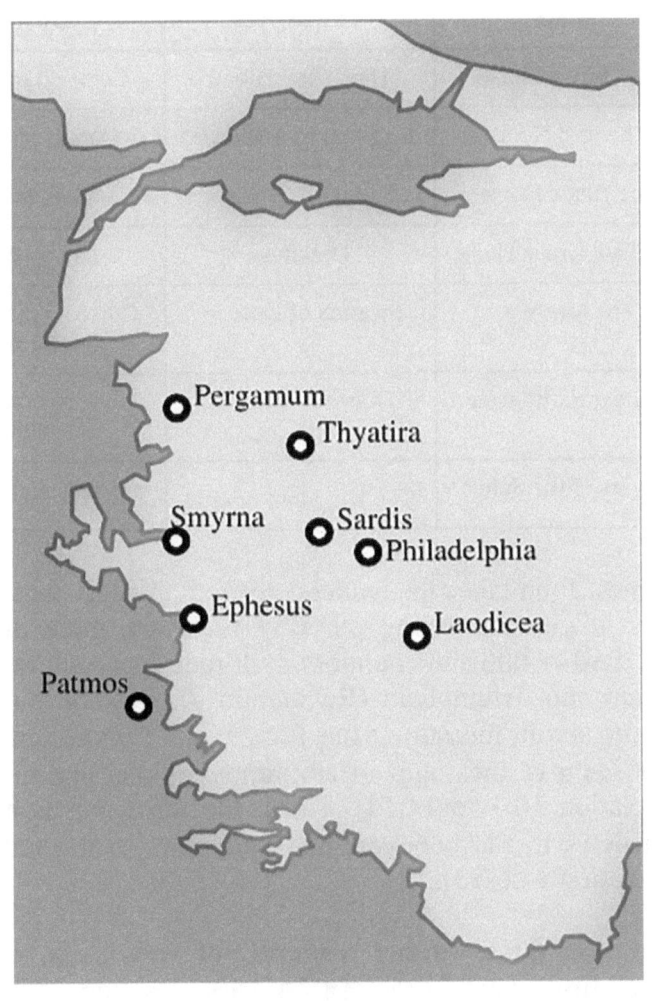

*Seven Churches of Roman Asia
& Patmos in the Aegean Sea*

Seals	Trumpets	Bowls
The White Horse	Hail, Fire, Blood	Curse on the Earth
The Red Horse	Eruption of a Volcano	Curse on the Sea
The Black Horse	Pollution of Water	Curse on the Rivers
The Pale Green Horse	Darkness	Curse on the Sun
The Martyrs	Swarms of Locusts	Curse on the Throne of the Beast
A Great Earthquake	Troops of Cavalry	Curse on the Euphrates
Prayers of the Saints	The Kingdom of God	Curse on the Air

At times, John takes his readers close up to study the details of God's judgement. Along the way there are three interludes. First, the 144,000 and countless multitude represent the Church Militant and Triumphant (Revelation 7:1-17). Second, eating the little scroll, measuring the Temple and prophesying by two witnesses give messages of assurance to John and his readers (Revelation 10:1 to 11:14). Third, the three angels announce good news to the believers and bad news to the unbelievers (Revelation 14:6-13).

There are three further patterns of seven: seven sights (Revelation 12:1-14:5; 14:14-15:4), seven judgements (Revelation 17:1-20:3) and seven promises (Revelation 20:4-22:5).

Sights	Judgements	Promises
Woman, Child, Dragon	The Great Whore	The Thousand Years
Beast from the Sea	The Great City	The Judgement of Evil
Beast from the Land	The Marriage of the Lamb	New Heaven & New Earth
The Lamb & the Church	The Word of God	Their God & My Children
The Son of Man	The Angel in the Sun	The Holy City
Harvest of Grapes	The Beast's Defeat	The Light of the City
The Song of the Lamb	The Devil's Imprisonment	The River of Life

John's conclusion emphasises the authenticity of his message and the imminence of God's judgement (Revelation 22:6-21). For example, the angel says, *"These words are trustworthy and true"* and Jesus says, *"See, I am coming soon!"* (Revelation 22:6-7)

Promises in the Book of Revelation

Chapters 2 and 3 contains promises to 'conquerors' or 'victors':
- The Tree of Life — Revelation 2:7
- The Crown of Life — Revelation 2:11
- The Bread of Heaven — Revelation 2:17
- The Victory of God — Revelation 2:26-28
- The Book of Life — Revelation 3:5
- The Temple of God — Revelation 3:12
- The Throne of God — Revelation 3:21

The promises belong to the faithful in anticipation of the ultimate victory of God.

Blessings in the Book of Revelation

Scattered throughout Revelation are blessings that take us beyond the secret codes of John to the absolute certainties of Christ:

The Reader and the Hearers	Revelation 1:3
The Faithful Dead	Revelation 14:13
The Sentinel	Revelation 16:15
The Guests	Revelation 19:9
The Holy and Hopeful	Revelation 20:6
The Obedient	Revelation 22:7
The Cleansed	Revelation 22:14

The blessings, like the promises, belong to the faithful who trust in Jesus the Redeemer and the victory of God the Creator.

Christian Martyrs of the Twentieth Century

Throughout our treatment of the promises and blessings in the Revelation to John, we consider ten martyrs of the twentieth century. The life, thought and death of all ten are featured on separate pages. These martyrs are examples of countless followers of Jesus who gave their lives in the face of injustice, repression, bigotry, authoritarianism, zealotry, violence and insanity. All of this happened in a century marked by the rise of dictators, two world wars, so called lesser wars, genocide, the creation of one party states, the entrapment of minorities and horror after horror. The message of the Revelation to John remains strangely relevant.

Ancient and modern readers of the book of Revelation would identify with the ten individual martyrs whose statues are on the west front of Westminster Abbey. They lived out and died for the abiding message of John the Seer on the Isle of Patmos. The triumphant end is certain because it has already begun through God's action in Christ; it is now known through God's presence among his people; and it will be concluded in God's time in the personal presence of Christ in the new heavens and the new earth.

The ten statues above the west door of Westminster Abbey represent individual martyrs who died for their faith. Included are victims of the struggle for human rights, of the Soviet and Nazi persecutions, of religious prejudice, of dictatorial rule, of antichristian fanaticism, of wartime brutality and of revolutionary madness. The ten martyrs represent all continents and many Christian denominations. These people died for their faith in Christ. They are modern examples of Tertullian's words, 'The blood of the martyrs is the seed of the church.'

Year	Martyr	Country	L>R
1918	Grand Duchess Elizabeth	Russia	4
1928	Manche Masemola	South Africa	2
1941	Maximilian Kolbe	Poland	1
1942	Lucian Tapiedi	Papua New Guinea	9
1945	Dietrich Bonhoeffer	Germany	7
1960	Esther John	Pakistan	8
1968	Martin Luther King	United States	5
1972	Wang Zhiming	China	10
1977	Janani Luwum	Uganda	3
1980	Oscar Romero	El Salvadore	6

PROMISES
in the Book of Revelation

Patmos

1 The Tree of Life

The letter to the church in Ephesus has as its key the idea of love. Christ admonishes us to love God and neighbour and promises that we, as conquerors, shall eat the fruits of the tree of life.

> *To everyone who conquers,*
> *I will give permission to eat from the tree of life*
> *that is in the paradise of God.*
> *(Revelation 2:7)*

Context

To the angel of the church in Ephesus write. (2:1a)

Ephesus has been called 'the vanity fair of the ancient world'. It was the western terminus to the Roman road system with three major routes from the River Euphrates. According to an ancient writer, it was the greatest emporium in Asia. It was a place where you could shop until you drop! Ephesus had a population of 200,000. It had a magnificent outdoor theatre and a long marble main street with temples and monuments. The city was the most important harbour in Asia Minor and was dominated by the temple of Artemis (Greek) or Diana (Latin).

Today the harbour is a reed-bed and Ephesus, but not the temple of Artemis, is a well preserved ruin. In the area are the traditional sites of the tombs of John the apostle and Mary the mother of Jesus. Today many tourists come from Kusadasi on the coast of the Aegean Sea to visit Ephesus, which is indeed the best preserved Roman city in the eastern Mediterranean region. The modern town of Selçuk has benefited from its proximity to Ephesus and has many places for tourists to stay.

Christ

These are the words of him who holds the seven stars in his right hand, who walks among the seven golden lampstands. (2:1b)

The seven stars have been interpreted as guardian angels or congregational leaders or symbols of heavenly counterparts of the earthly congregations. The seven lampstands are symbols of the seven churches. Just as Ephesus the seaport is the centre of the seven cities in terms of trade and commerce, so Jesus is the centre of attention for the churches in the cities. The unseen Christ walks among the churches. He inspects the churches. He calls the churches to account.

Commendation

I know your works, your toil and your patient endurance. I know that you cannot tolerate evildoers; you have tested those who claim to be apostles but are not, and have found them to be false. I also know that you are enduring patiently and bearing up for the sake of my name, and that you have not grown weary. (2:2-3)

The Ephesian Christians are commended for their toil in maintaining true faith in the face of false teachers and for their endurance in following Jesus despite the temptation to give up. They are not 'all talk and no action'. Notice the active words of praise: works, toil, endurance, bearing up, not growing weary.

Criticism

But I have this against you, that you have abandoned the love you had at first. Remember then from what you have fallen; repent, and do the works you did at first. If not, I will come to you and remove your lampstand from its place, unless you repent. Yet this is to your credit: you hate the works of the Nicolaitans, which I also hate. (2:4-6)

The Ephesian Christians are criticised for their loss of love. Where love for God decreases, love for people diminishes, and where love for people is embittered, love for God is reduced to religious formalism, and both deny the reality of God in Jesus, the man for others.

The Nicolaitans are probably early gnostics, people with special knowledge, teaching that body and soul are separate and that what one does with the body does not affect the soul. How wrong they are! The Ephesian Christians are advised to keep remembering God's love, to repent of their lovelessness and to become active again. The Christian's walk and talk belong together.

Conqueror

Let anyone who has an ear listen to what the Spirit is saying to the churches. To everyone who conquers, I will give permission to eat from the tree of life that is in the paradise of God. (2:7)

The Christian life is a warfare from which there is no let up. However, it is a battle in which even the feeblest follower of Jesus can be victorious. Every faithful believer is promised that paradise lost will be paradise regained.

First of all the Bible tells the story of paradise lost. *And the LORD God planted a garden in Eden, in the east; and there he put the man whom he had formed ... He drove out the man; and at the east of the garden of Eden he placed the cherubim, and a sword flaming and turning to guard the way to the tree of life. (Genesis 2:8; 3:24)*

Last of all the Bible tells the story of paradise regained. *Then the angel showed me the river of the water of life, bright as crystal, flowing from the throne of God and of the Lamb through the middle of the street of the city. On either side of the river is the tree of life with its twelve kinds of fruit, producing its fruit each month; and the leaves of the tree are for the healing of the nations. (Revelation 22:1-2)*

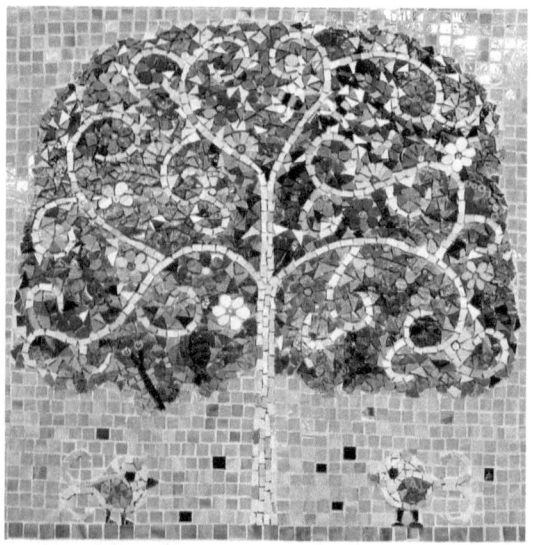

Today's artisans in Turkey produce beautiful carpets in wool or silk featuring the tree of life. In the letter to Ephesus the tree of life has two other associations.

First, the temple of Artemis had at its centre a tree. It marked the place of an asylum for unrepentant criminals. Second, the story of Jesus led to his death on a tree. It marked the place of refuge for repentant sinners. God gives us victory over evil and death through his crucified and risen Son.

The promise to the one who is conquering is to eat from the tree of life in Revelation 2:7. This is fulfilled at the end of the book in the words of Revelation 22:2, *On either side of the river [of the water of life] is the tree of life with its twelve kinds of fruit, producing its fruit each month; and the leaves of the tree are for the healing of the nations.*

Connections

A colleague of mine left a school chaplaincy to become a church minister. I was a teacher of religious education in a secondary school. He asked for some advice. I offered a suggestion: 'Preach the word of God and love your people.' A month after he took up the position I saw him again and I asked him whether my advice was any help. Fortunately he was positive. 'Yes,' he said, 'you got it right.'

Outstanding Scottish preacher James S. Stewart noted that the body of Christ results from four historical acts: the Incarnation, the Cross, the Resurrection and the Day of Pentecost. He asked whether the people of God can measure up to any of these descriptions 'with penitence and contrition'. Professor Stewart was aware that Jesus didn't send someone else to pull us up, but came himself. He became one of us and lived among us. As the Fourth Gospel put it, *the Word became flesh and lived among us*, and *God so loved the world that he gave his only Son. (John 1:14; 3:16)* Therefore, in the words of the First Letter of John, *We love because he first loved us. (1 John 4:19)*

Grand Duchess Elizabeth

is a saint of the Russian Orthodox Church. During the Russian Communist Revolution she was killed by the Bolsheviks in 1918.

Named after a Roman Catholic saint, baptized as a child into the Lutheran Church, brought up as a teenager in an Anglican home with her grandmother Queen Victoria, married to the Russian Orthodox fifth son of the Czar, Elizabeth experienced the assassination of her husband in 1905.

Elizabeth founded the Community of Mary and Martha, Sisters of the Cross of Love and Mercy, for the service of the poor and needy.

On the day of their dedication, she said, *'I am leaving a glittering world where I had a glittering position, but with all of you I am descending into a greater world - the world of the poor and the suffering.'*

Because Elizabeth was German on her father's side, English on her mother's, and Russian by marriage, she faced suspicion during the Great War. When the Czar was overthrown, she suffered at the hands of revolutionary forces and died a day after the Russian royal family was killed.

Her remains were finally buried in the crypt below the Russian Church of St Mary Magdalene above the Garden of Gethsemane in Jerusalem.

2 The Crown of Life

The letter to the church at Smyrna has as its key the idea of suffering. Christ reminds us of the need to persevere and promises that we, as conquerors, shall have immunity from annihilation.

Whoever conquers will not be harmed by the second death. (Revelation 2:11)

Context

And to the angel of the church in Smyrna write. (2:8a)

Smyrna has been called 'the glory of Asia'. Coins described the city as 'first of Asia in beauty and size'. The city was fifty-six kilometres (thirty-five miles) north of Ephesus. Smyrna was the birthplace of Homer. It had a population of 200,000. The original city had been destroyed about 600 BC and was rebuilt in 290 BC. In New Testament times Smyrna was a centre of emperor worship and had a large Jewish population.

The city's allegiance to Rome and its large Jewish community led to persecution and martyrdom of Christians. The most famous martyr was Polycarp in the second century. As he was about to die he testified, 'For eighty-six years I have served him, and he has done me no wrong; how can I blaspheme my King who saved me?' Modern Izmir covers most of ancient Smyrna. Except for the marketplace, theatre and sections of the Roman aqueduct, little remains of ancient Smyrna. Izmir is Turkey's major port on the Aegean Sea and its third largest city with a population of 2,000,000.

Christ

These are the words of the first and the last, who was dead and came to life. (2:8b)

The description of Jesus *the first and the last* echoes Isaiah of Babylon. *Thus says the LORD, the King of Israel, and his Redeemer, the LORD of hosts: I am the first and I am the last; besides me there is no god. (Isaiah 44:6) Listen to me, O Jacob, and Israel, whom I called: I am He; I am the first, and I am the last. (Isaiah 48:12)*

The description of Jesus *who was dead and came to life* also echoes the history of Smyrna: destroyed in 600 BC and rebuilt in 290 BC. However, it only took Jesus three days to die and to rise again! He plunged into death and sprang to life.

Commendation

I know your affliction and your poverty, even though you are rich. I know the slander on the part of those who say that they are Jews and are not, but are a synagogue of Satan. Do not fear what you are about to suffer. Beware, the devil is about to throw some of you into prison so that you may be tested, and for ten days you will have affliction. (2:9-10a)

The plight of the Christians of Smyrna, poor materially yet rich spiritually, is opposite to the plight of the Christians of Laodicea rich materially yet poor spiritually. The Christians of Smyrna face their affliction, poverty and slander admirably. They confront suffering in the knowledge that their Lord also suffered. Unfortunately, the Christians of Smyrna face opposition. A parting of the ways between Jews and Christians is occurring.

It is probable that Polycarp was an active follower of Jesus in Smyrna when John wrote to the church at Smyrna. Forty years after the writing of Revelation, Polycarp had become the leader of the Christians at Smyrna. In AD 135 some Jews at Smyrna participated in the denunciation and the death of Polycarp.

Therefore, a long standing state of enmity may explain why John calls hostile Jews at Smyrna *a synagogue of Satan*. The Christians of Smyrna are warned of ten days of affliction. The figure is symbolic of a complete period. The period represents real suffering as witnesses to Jesus but is restricted by God.

In Genesis 22 God asks Abraham to sacrifice his only son Isaac. There is an interesting retelling by the rabbis. Abraham asks God: 'Why did I have to undergo this experience? Did you need a test to determine my faithfulness?' God replies, 'No.' Abraham says, 'Did I need a test to prove my own faithfulness?' God answers, 'No.' 'Why did I have to go through this experience?' Abraham asks. God replies, 'As a witness to the nations.' Witnessing sons and daughters of Abraham by faith, whether they were Jew or Gentile, could identify with the rabbis' story.

Criticism

There is no criticism! The Christians of Smyrna suffer for their faith. They depend radically on God and obey his will. It is true that suffering reminds us of the things in life which really matter.

Conqueror

Be faithful until death, and I will give you the crown of life. Let anyone who has an ear listen to what the Spirit is saying to the churches. Whoever conquers will not be harmed by the second death. (2:10b, 11)

The promise to every faithful believer is positive, *Be faithful until death, and I will give you the crown of life*, and negative, *Whoever conquers will not be harmed by the second death.*

The idea of *the crown of life* is paralleled by the words of Paul as he faces the end of his life in 2 Timothy 4:7-8, *I have fought the good fight, I have finished the race, I have kept the faith. From now on there is reserved for me the crown of righteousness, which the Lord, the righteous judge, will give me on that day, and not only to me but also to all who have longed for his appearing.* The crown is the laurel wreath worn by winners in the Greek and Roman games.

The picture of *the crown of life* is also a reminder of a crown of beautiful buildings and a street of gold in Smyrna. As people looked at Smyrna they would have seen the city rising in symmetry to a crown of battlements which served as a safe haven in time of war. The crown of the earthly Smyrna is implicitly compared with the crown of the heavenly Jerusalem. The former is surpassed by the latter.

The Jewish idea of *the second death* means either people do not qualify for resurrection or people suffer judgement in the world to come. There is a provocative badge worn by some brave believers, 'Born once, die twice. Born twice, die once.' God cannot promise immunity from the death which kills the body, but he can promise immunity from that which annihilates the soul.

The promise to the conqueror of receiving the crown of life and not being harmed by the second death in Revelation 2:10,11 is fulfilled towards the end of the book in the words of Revelation 20:6, *Blessed and holy are those who share in the first resurrection. Over these the second death has no power, but they will be priests of God and of Christ, and they will reign with him a thousand years.*

Connections

As Professor James Stewart once said, 'The New Testament is not a dull treatise on ethical theism or mild humanitarianism or respectable behaviour. It is much more like a wild treasure island story, throbbing with exhilaration of stupendous discovery, fabulous wealth, colossal unsearchable riches ... God bears the sins of the world ... Christ communicates life ...'

The letter to the Christians at Smyrna is challenging but encouraging. As we shall see, they share with the Christians at Philadelphia the joy of hearing Christ speak to them with commendation and without criticism.

The experience of the first century church at Smyrna has a message for members of the churches of the twenty-first century. It is one thing to say that Jesus saves us from our sins. It is another thing to say that Jesus is our Lord and owns everything we have. Becoming a Christian includes being a Christian. Conversion involves both an initial decision and a lifelong process.

Manche Masemola

was a South African sixteen year old who became a Christian. She was killed by her animist parents of the Pedi tribe.

Manche was born about 1912 in the Transvaal. She grew up with her parents, two older brothers, a younger sister and a cousin named Lucia.

When she was thirteen, Manche went with Lucia and heard an Anglican Missionary preach at Marishane. She began to attend Christian classes twice a week. Her parents tried to discourage her. She was told to attend the tribal initiation school. But Manche continued to go to the Christian classes.

Her parents attempted to arrange a marriage for her with a young man of their tribe. They even resorted to repeated beatings of the young girl to discourage her interest in Christianity.

The Anglican missionary remembered Manche saying, *'If they cut off my head, I will never leave my faith.'* The last time he saw her she said to him, *'I shall be baptized with my own blood.'* Her cousin was sent away due to her supposedly bad influence.

On February 4, 1928 Manche's parents took her to a lonely place and beat her to death. A fortnight later her sister became ill and died. She was buried beside Manche. In 1969 her mother was baptized into the church. She had been won over to faith in Christ by the hope, perseverance and fortitude of her martyred daughter.

3 The Bread of Heaven

The letter to the church at Pergamum has as its key the idea of truth. Christ reminds us to be aware of the dangers of false teachers and promises that we, as conquerors, shall feed on the bread of heaven for evermore.

> *To everyone who conquers*
> *I will give some of the hidden manna,*
> *and I will give a white stone,*
> *and on the white stone is written a new name*
> *that no one knows*
> *except the one who receives it.*
> *(Revelation 2:17)*

Context

And to the angel of the church in Pergamum write. (2:12a)

Pergamum has been called 'the most illustrious city of Asia'. The city was seventy-two kilometres (forty-five miles) north of Smyrna. Pergamum had a population of 120,000. This city was built up a hill. Its name means 'citadel'. Pergamum was a pioneer of town planning and zoning. It was a centre of the worship of Asclepius (the serpent god of healing). Indeed, Pergamum could be called the Lourdes of the ancient world. It was also a centre of the worship of Zeus (the king of the Greek gods) and the Roman emperors. Nero identified himself as 'Saviour and Lord'. Domitian claimed to be 'Lord and God'.

Pergamum was famous for its library of 200,000 books and its development of parchment. The word 'parchment' comes from the Greek name of Pergamum. Modern Bergama, at the foot of the ruins of ancient Pergamum, today has a population of 50,000 and is a farmers' market town in the middle of a well-watered plain.

Christ

These are the words of him who has the sharp two-edged sword. (2:12b)

Pergamum was called the city of the sword due to the power of its senate to inflict the death penalty. The implication of the description of Jesus as *him who has the sharp two-edged sword* is that the sword of the Son of Man is far greater than the famous sword of Pergamum. Jesus the Lord administers the justice of God.

Commendation

I know where you are living, where Satan's throne is. Yet you are holding fast to my name, and you did not deny your faith in me even in the days of Antipas my witness, my faithful one, who was killed among you, where Satan lives. (2:13)

Given that Pergamum was a centre of the worship of Asclepius, Zeus and the Emperor, the Christians in the city knew that it was *where Satan's throne is . . . where Satan lives.* Even so, they hold fast and do not deny their faith. That is high praise.

We don't know anything else about Antipas. He is described as a witness to Jesus and a faithful follower of Jesus. The Greek word translated *witness* is *martys*. This may be one of the first times it was used to signify a martyr. Antipas seems to have been a witness to Jesus at the cost of his life.

Criticism

But I have a few things against you: you have some there who hold to the teaching of Balaam, who taught Balak to put a stumbling block before the people of Israel, so that they would eat food sacrificed to idols and practice fornication. So you also have some who hold to the teaching of the Nicolaitans. Repent then. If not, I will come to you soon and make war against them with the sword of my mouth. (2:14-16)

It appears that the Christians in Pergamum are tempted to sacrifice to idols and to practise fornication. This means that they could be accused of either literal sexual immorality or idolatry in a metaphorical sense as infidelity to God.

Balaam and Balak feature in Numbers 25:1-2; 31:16 and Jude 11. They were understood to have led the Israelites astray into idolatry and immorality. Holding to the teaching of the Nicolaitans is the same as holding to the teaching of Balaam.

The church at Pergamum is hanging on, even hanging loose. Tolerant Pergamum is the opposite of intolerant Ephesus. Whereas Pergamum is told, *you also have some who hold to the teaching of the Nicolaitans (Revelation 2:15)*, Ephesus was told, *Yet this is to your credit: you hate the works of the Nicolaitans, which I also hate (Revelation 2:6)*.

Conqueror

Let anyone who has an ear listen to what the Spirit is saying to the churches. To everyone who conquers I will give some of the hidden manna, and I will give a white stone, and on the white stone is written a new name that no one knows except the one who receives it. (2:17)

The promise to every faithful believer includes three things, which many have clung on to as they find themselves spiritually hungry in an alien environment.

First is *the hidden manna* which is the bread of heaven. In the Fourth Gospel the bread of God is Jesus who says, *I am the bread of life. Whoever comes to me will never be hungry, and whoever believes in me will never be thirsty ... This is the bread that came down from heaven, not like that which your ancestors ate, and they died. But the one who eats this bread will live forever. (John 6:35, 58)* At Pergamum the Nicolaitans probably are eating food sacrificed to idols and face judgement by the sword of the Lord. On the other hand, the Christians will eat the bread of heaven and await vindication by the coming king.

Second is *a white stone* which could be one of three things. A white stone indicated acquittal by a jury at a trial. It also was a ticket of admission to a public occasion such as a festival. It also was a magical amulet or charm for pagan cults. Perhaps the white stone reminds followers of Jesus that he puts them in the right with God, invites them to the messianic feast in the new heaven and new earth, and protects them from the power of evil.

Third is *a new name* written on the white stone. The new name is either the name of a believer - who has become a Christian - or is the name of the Saviour - Christ is Lord of all, not Caesar - and as a result, there is a new life in Christ the Lord. One is reminded of the words of Paul: *If anyone is in Christ, there is a new creation: everything old has passed away; see, everything has become new! (2 Corinthians 5:17)*

The promise to the conqueror of receiving the hidden manna, the white stone, and the new name in Revelation 2:17 is not explicitly fulfilled at the end of the book of Revelation. However, Revelation 3:12, in the letter to the church at Philadelphia, picks up the theme of a new name: *I will write on you the name of my God, and the name of the city of my God, the new Jerusalem that comes down from my God out of heaven, and my own new name.*

Connections

The experience of the first century church at Pergamum has two lessons for the churches of the twenty-first century.

First is a warning. Albert Schweitzer in his magnum opus, *The Quest of the Historical Jesus,* noted the watering down of the great imperious sayings of Jesus. As he said, 'Many of the greatest sayings are found lying in a corner like explosive shells from which the charges have been removed.'

Second is an encouragement. William E. Hull, eloquent preacher and gifted professor, said it well: 'Jesus was right: tragedy is but the raw material of hope, the dark backdrop against which it is possible to glimpse the glory of God.' 'Tragedy is not redeemed by being explained but by being changed!'

Maximilian Kolbe

is a saint of the Roman Catholic Church. He was killed by the Nazis in 1941.

Kolbe was born in Poland in 1894 to parents who had a living faith and a spirit of patriotism. His father was killed by the Russians at the beginning of the Great War.

When he was eighteen Maximilian went to Rome to study philosophy and theology. He became devoted to the Virgin Mary and worked to win converts and to do good deeds. On his return to Poland he lectured at a Franciscan seminary. Then he spent six years in Nagasaki, Japan, before returning to Poland to work in a publishing house.

When the Second World War broke out, Kolbe was interned and eventually became an inmate of Auschwitz. Even though his own health deteriorated, he gave away his own food to other prisoners. Despite the strictures of the concentration camp, he celebrated mass and heard confessions.

A prisoner's escape led the Nazi commandant to order the death of ten other prisoners by starvation. When one of the ten wept and spoke of his wife and children, Maximilian said, *'I want to die in place of this prisoner.'* He was allowed to do so. In the starvation cell six of the ten died within a fortnight. He was fully conscious when he was killed by lethal injection on August 14, 1941.

4 The Victory of God

The letter to the church at Thyatira has as its key the idea of holiness. Christ makes us think of our faith in reference to our life-style and promises that we shall participate in the ultimate victory of God.

> *To everyone who conquers*
> *and continues to do my works to the end,*
> *I will give authority over the nations;*
> *to rule them with an iron rod,*
> *as when clay pots are shattered —*
> *even as I also received authority from my Father.*
> *To the one who conquers*
> *I will also give the morning star.*
> *(Revelation 2:26-28)*

Context

And to the angel of the church in Thyatira write. (2:18a)

The longest letter in Revelation 2 and 3 is addressed to Thyatira sixty-four kilometres (forty miles) south east of Pergamum. Thyatira has been described as 'the least known, least important and least remarkable' of the seven cities in Roman Asia. However, it was known for its clothing industry and trade guilds. The city was a centre of the wool trade and the dyeing industry. Thyatira could be called a trade union town, the Broken Hill of the ancient world. The guilds of Thyatira had three features: their religious basis, their apparent localisation and their continuing existence.

According to Acts 16:14-15, Lydia, a convert of Paul at Philippi, was a representative of the Thyatira purple cloth industry. Tyrimnos, the god of Thyatira, was identified with both the sun god Apollo and the emperor Domitian. Modern Akhisar (meaning 'white castle') covers ancient Thyatira.

Christ

These are the words of the Son of God, who has eyes like a flame of fire, and whose feet are like burnished bronze. (2:18b)

As we have noted, the god of Thyatira was identified with the sun god Apollo and the emperor Domitian. The picture of *the Son of God, who has eyes like a flame of fire, and whose feet are like burnished bronze* is probably stated in similar terms to oppose the combination of the local religion with the imperial religion. Jesus the Messiah with *eyes like a flame of fire* can see through the compromises of the Thyatiran Christians and with *feet like burnished bronze* has strength to judge their pagan opponents. Christ is the King not Caesar.

Commendation

I know your works — your love, faith, service, and patient endurance. I know that your last works are greater than the first. (2:19)

Whereas the Christians of Ephesus are praised for their *toil* and *patient endurance* (but they are criticised for their decreasing love), the Thyatiran Christians are praised for their increasing *love, faith, service, and patient endurance*. They are going from strength to strength. Motivated by love and faith they serve and endure patiently. Nevertheless, all is not well with the followers of Jesus in Thyatira.

Criticism

But I have this against you: you tolerate that woman Jezebel, who calls herself a prophet and is teaching and beguiling my servants to practise fornication and to eat food sacrificed to idols. I gave her time to repent, but she refuses to repent of her fornication. Beware, I am throwing her on a bed, and those who commit adultery with her I am throwing into great distress, unless they repent of her doings; and I will strike her children dead. And all the churches will know that I am the one who searches minds and hearts, and I will give to each of you as your works deserve. But to the rest of you in Thyatira, who do not hold this teaching, who have not learned what some call 'the deep things of Satan,' to you I say, I do not lay on you any other burden; only hold fast to what you have until I come. (2:20-25)

The phrase *the deep things of Satan* probably indicates that the Thyatiran Christians consciously free themselves from traditional ethics and boldly engage in fashionable religious expression. *Jezebel* of Samaria features in 1 Kings 16:31 and 2 Kings 9:22. She was understood to have led Ahab the northern king astray into idolatry and immorality. Elijah the prophet was her great antagonist.

Jezebel of Thyatira is probably encouraging the people to participate in sexual rites in the local worship centres, to eat meat offered to idols, and even to worship at the statue of Caesar Domitian. She claims special knowledge which gives freedom in the spiritual world in both heaven and hell. But *the one who searches minds and hearts* will give to all their just desserts.

Thyatira is a church that is tempted to compromise with their message and mission. Today's equivalent would be the difficult challenge of reconciling the claims of Christian life with the claims of working and social life. How far do we go in being faithful to Christ and in making concessions to work and society?

Conqueror

To everyone who conquers and continues to do my works to the end, I will give authority over the nations; to rule them with an iron rod, as when clay pots are shattered — even as I also received authority from my Father. To the one who conquers I will also give the morning star. Let anyone who has an ear listen to what the Spirit is saying to the churches. (2:26-29)

The promise to every faithful believer includes two things. First is *authority over the nations* which is the power to crush the opposing forces of paganism. The first part of the promise is based on a messianic reading of Psalm 2:8-9. The message of Christ to the church at Thyatira is that pagan resistance will certainly be smashed, but God will use no other iron bar than the death of his Son and the martyrdom of his saints.

Second is *the morning star* which is the planet Venus as a symbol of victory and sovereignty. The second part of the promise may be based on a messianic reading of Numbers 24:17. It has also been suggested that as Venus is the last star to set, so the follower of Jesus should be the last person to give in.

The first part of the promise, *authority over the nations*, is fulfilled in the words of Revelation 20:4, 6, *Then I saw thrones, and those seated on them were given authority to judge ... They came to life and reigned with Christ a thousand years ... Blessed and holy are those who share in the first resurrection ... and they will reign with him a thousand years.*

The second part of the promise, *the morning star*, is fulfilled in the words of Jesus in Revelation 22:16, *It is I, Jesus, who sent my angel to you with this testimony for the churches. I am the root and the descendant of David, the bright morning star.*

Connections

The church at Thyatira is tempted to compromise. They forget that their talk has to be proved in their walk. Sometimes it's hard to do what we say we should do. It's a case of 'We can talk the walk, but can we walk the talk?' One thinks of Dietrich Bonhoeffer's concept of 'cheap grace'. Whereas costly grace is the call to commitment, cheap grace is forgiveness without repentance, baptism without discipline and communion without confession.

The church at Thyatira is challenged to do brave deeds and endure. It is as though Jesus is telling them, and us, to hang on until he comes. We can remember times that we have hung on until someone came to relieve us at work or at home or at a social occasion. Such experiences remind us that an effective way of resisting temptation is to keep recalling that Jesus is coming. His coming may be in the experiences of life or at the end of life as we know it.

Lucian Tapiedi

was a Papuan convert who became an Anglican evangelist. He was killed during the Japanese invasion in 1942.

Born in 1921, he was the son of a sorcerer. After his father's death his mother became a Christian. Lucian attended mission schools from the age of 10. He came to personal faith two years later. He studied at a church teacher training college between 1939 and 1941. He worked as a teacher and evangelist at a mission school. he was intelligent, enthusiastic, friendly, sporting and musical.

When the Japanese invaded Papua, Lucian decided not to leave the missionaries with whom he worked. He said, *'I will stay with the Fathers and Sisters.'*

During the Second World War 333 Christians died as martyrs in Papua New Guinea. They sacrificed their lives to do Christ's work in the face of the invaders. Most died at the hands of the invaders. Lucian was actually killed by a man of another tribe.

A cairn of stones marks the place of his death. His murderer was later converted and assumed the name of Lucian in baptism. Lucian the martyr helped break down the image of Christianity as European and set an example of indigenous church leadership.

5 The Book of Life

The letter to the church at Sardis has as its key the idea of reality. Christ promises us, if we accept God's ways and stay alert in working for Christ, that our names will be remain in the book of life.

> *If you conquer,*
> *you will be clothed like them in white robes,*
> *and I will not blot your name out of the book of life;*
> *I will confess your name*
> *before my Father and before his angels.*
> *(Revelation 3:5)*

Context

And to the angel of the church in Sardis write. (3:1a)

Sardis has been described as a city of 'an easy and voluptuous decadence'. The city was forty-eight kilometres (thirty miles) south of Thyatira. It had a population of 100,000. One part of Sardis was in the valley, the other part was on top of Mount Tmoulos. It reached the peak of its prosperity under Croesus in 560 BC. According to legend, everything Croesus touched turned to gold. Twice Sardis had been captured by invading kings, Cyrus in 546 BC and Antiochus in 218 BC. Both came like thieves in the night. The city was a centre of pagan worship for Cybele, also known as Artemis. It was also a centre of Jewish worship with a large synagogue. Sardis won fame for the manufacture of white cloth by its fabric industry.

An earthquake devastated the city in AD 17 but it had recovered by AD 26. Modern Sart is nearby the ruins of ancient

Sardis. To the east are the ruins of the temple of Artemis, to the west are ancient tombs called 'The City of the Dead'. Modern Sart consists of two small villages, one on the highway and the other around the railway station, in a valley of vineyards, olive groves, melon gardens and tobacco fields.

Christ

These are the words of him who has the seven spirits of God and the seven stars. (3:1b)

Jesus the Messiah holds *the seven spirits of God and the seven stars.* The *seven spirits* represent the Holy Spirit given in his fullness to the churches at Ephesus, Smyrna, Pergamum, Thyatira, Sardis, Philadelphia and Laodicea. The *seven stars* can be interpreted as guardian angels or congregational leaders or symbols of heavenly counterparts of the earthly congregations.

Commendation

There is no commendation! It appears that the church at Sardis was not troubled by persecution from outside or by heresy from within. Here is a church which everyone speaks well of. The church at Sardis is perfectly inoffensive, completely innocuous, not worth worrying about! Sardis is a case of all show and no substance. The criticism that follows gives a devastating diagnosis of the church's present condition. They have a reputation of being alive but a reality of being 'The City of the Dead'.

Criticism

I know your works; you have a name of being alive, but you are dead. Wake up, and strengthen what remains and is on the point of death, for I have not found your works perfect in the sight of my God. Remember then what you received and heard; obey it, and repent. If you do not wake up, I will come like a thief, and you will not know at what hour I will come to you. Yet you have still a few persons in Sardis who have not soiled their clothes; they will walk with me, dressed in white, for they are worthy. (3:1c-4)

The Christians of Sardis resemble the city of Sardis. They are wishy washy, they are not motivated, they suffer from inertia, they are content with mediocrity. No other city in the region presents such a deplorable contrast of past splendour and present decline. Unfortunately, the church is no different from the city.

In a city which had twice been taken unawares and captured by enemies, Cyrus the Persian and Alexander the Great, the church faces judgement! In a city which featured a cemetery called 'The City of the Dead', the church could be called 'The Community of the Spiritually Dead'! In a city famous for its white cloth the church is infamous for its dirty linen! No wonder that the church is told to wake up, strengthen, remember, obey and repent! The church at Sardis certainly needs to start again.

Conqueror

If you conquer, you will be clothed like them in white robes, and I will not blot your name out of the book of life; I will confess your name before my Father and before his angels. Let anyone who has an ear listen to what the Spirit is saying to the churches. (3:5-6)

The promise to every faithful believer includes two things. First is being *clothed in white robes* which are the unsoiled garments of faithful and pure believers. As Roman citizens used to don white robes at the triumphal procession of an emperor, so will Christian believers be *clothed in white robes* when the Lord Jesus is acknowledged as supreme. The imagery of Christ's triumphal procession is found in 2 Corinthians 2:14 and Colossians 2:15.

Second is having their *names in the book of life* which is the register of the citizens of the heavenly kingdom. The names have been in the book of life from the foundation of the world(Revelation 17:8) and belong to the citizens of the new heaven and the new earth (Revelation 21:27). The right to have one's *name in the book of life* cannot be earned but it can be forfeited. As Ben Witherington often says, 'One is not eternally secure until one is securely in eternity.'

Connections

The short but sad letter to Sardis leads to an observation by James S. Stewart. We can have all the nominal Christianity in the world, but if we do not have the life of Jesus, we are nothing. When we wake up to experience the risen Christ, the nothingness of nominal Christianity will give way to the meaningfulness of real faith, hope and love as he renews our lives and enrols our names in the book of new life.

The musical play *My Fair Lady* has a memorable song. Freddy is trying to win Eliza's heart. She tells him why he is unsuccessful by singing, 'Words! Words! Words! Don't talk of love! Show me! Show me! Show me!' Christ awaits not only to hear our words but to see our deeds.

If our words are matched by our deeds, we are entitled to be in the company of the followers of Jesus, to be the saints of God. The word 'saints' is not to be confined to a select few; it includes all Christians who are meant to be dedicated or consecrated to the service of God.

The Quaker mystic, Douglas Steere, listed six qualities of saints:

> First, they are Jesus' people whose lives have been recipients of God's grace and who put themselves at God's disposal. Saints are motivated by the gift of God in Jesus.
> Second, they are Jesus' people who seek not to be safe but to be faithful to God. Saints go out of their way to love God with heart, soul, mind, strength, and to love their neighbour as themselves.
> Third, they are Jesus' people who learn to cope with adversity. Saints are known for their tenacity in the face of difficulty.
> Fourth, they are Jesus' people who are joyful. Saints give thanks to God not for all circumstances but in all circumstances.
> Fifth, they are Jesus' people who not only have dreams but also seek to fulfil their dreams. Saints practise what they preach.
> Sixth, they are Jesus' people who are prayerful and pray constantly and unceasingly, consciously and unconsciously. Saints know that prayer is the Lord's abiding presence made real.

The church at Sardis reminds us of the need to be real saints.

Dietrich Bonhoeffer
was a German Lutheran pastor and theologian, killed by Hitler in 1945.

Bonhoeffer was born into an upper class family in 1906, his father an agnostic psychiatrist and his mother a grand daughter of a famous theologian. At thirteen, to his father's displeasure, he announced his intention to be a pastor. After school he was a student at Berlin University. During 1930-31 he studied in New York and was challenged by the vibrant faith of Black Baptists. His Swiss theological mentor, Karl Barth, had a profound impact on him. He rediscovered Luther's understanding of suffering disobedience in the face of priestly injustice.

In 1933-35 Dietrich served German speaking parishes in London. Back in Nazi Germany, he directed an illegal seminary until its closure by the Gestapo. In 1939, invited by Reinhold Niebuhr, he went to New York but then returned to Germany. He said, *'The way of Jesus Christ ... leads not from the world to God but from God to the world.'* Opposed to Hitler's regime, he was imprisoned in 1943.

A failed attempt to assassinate Hitler led to the execution of hundreds of political prisoners, including Bonhoeffer, who was hanged on April 9, 1945. Dietrich's last words testify to his hope in Christ: *'This is the end; for me the beginning of life!'*

6 The Temple of God

The letter to the church at Philadelphia has as its key the idea of opportunity. Christ tells us of the availability of an open door for ministry and promises that we, as conquerors, shall be pillars in the heavenly temple.

> *If you conquer,*
> *I will make you a pillar in the temple of my God;*
> *you will never go out of it.*
> *I will write on you the name of my God,*
> *and the name of the city of my God,*
> *the new Jerusalem that comes down from my God out of*
> *heaven, and my own new name.*
> *(Revelation 3:12)*

Context

And to the angel of the church in Philadelphia write. (3:7a)

Philadelphia has been called 'the missionary city'. It was forty-eight kilometres (thirty miles) south east of Sardis. Philadelphia was 'Little Athens'. It was founded to spread Greek culture, to inculcate loyalty to Greek kings, and to guard the eastern land routes. It suffered an earthquake in AD 17 and was slow to recover. In ancient times most of its population lived outside the city for fear of earthquakes. Its main god was Dionysius, the god of wine, and its main industry was wine production. In the 14th century Philadelphia stood alone as a Christian city against the Turks. Finally the Turks took it at the end of conflict between 1379 and 1390. It became the Muslim town of Alasehir, meaning 'the reddish city'. Modern Alasehir covers ancient Philadelphia.

Christ

These are the words of the holy one, the true one, who has the key of David, who opens and no one will shut, who shuts and no one opens. (3:7b)

Jesus is described as *the holy one, the true one, who has the key of David.* There are echoes of the book of Isaiah: God is called *the Holy One* (40:25) and *the key of the house of David* (22:22) is given to a faithful steward. There are also parallels in the Gospel of John where Jesus is identified as *the true light* (1:9) and *the true vine* (15:1). The holy and true one has the key to the kingdom of God. He opens the kingdom's door to people who accept him and shuts the kingdom's door to people who reject him.

God has given all authority to him in heaven and on earth. The followers of Jesus in all seven cities of Asia face the challenge to fulfill the great commission: *Go ... make disciples of all nations, baptizing them in the name of the Father and of the Son and of the Holy Spirit, and teaching them to obey everything that I have commanded you. (Matthew 28:19-20a)* As we shall see, the loyal Christians of Philadelphia are doing just that.

Commendation

I know your works. **Look**, *I have set before you an open door, which no one is able to shut. I know that you have but little power, and yet you have kept my word and have not denied my name.* **Look**, *I will make those of the synagogue of Satan who say that they are Jews and are not, but are lying —* **Look**, *I will make them come and bow down before your feet, and they will learn that I have loved you. Because you have kept my word of patient endurance, I will keep you from the hour of trial that is* *coming on the whole world to test the inhabitants of the earth. I am coming soon; hold fast to what you have, so that no one may seize your crown. (3:8-11)*

In the Greek this section uses a word which may be translated 'Behold!' or *Look!* (The NRSV only picks up the first occurrence. I have added the second and third occurrences.) The word draws attention to something being overlooked.

On the one hand, **Look**, *I have set before you an open door*. The Christians of Philadelphia may be encouraged by the thought that Christ has used the key of David to open the door which leads into the eternal kingdom. As Jesus the good shepherd said, *I am the gate. Whoever enters by me will be saved, and will come in and go out and find pasture. (John 10:9)* The Christians of Philadelphia may also be encouraged by the idea that God opens a door for the effective communication of the good news of Christ. Indeed, Paul wrote about when he stayed in Ephesus that *a wide door for effective work has opened to me (1 Corinthians 16:9)* and about when he came to Troas to preach the good news that *a door was opened for me in the Lord (2 Corinthians 2:12)*.

On the other hand, **Look**, *I will make those of the synagogue of Satan who say that they are Jews and are not, but are lying —* **Look**, *I will make them come and bow down before your feet, and they will learn that I have loved you.* The opponents of the Christians at Philadelphia, some hostile Jews, are called *the synagogue of Satan*. They negate the grace of true Judaism and the freedom of true Christianity. Even these opponents, *the synagogue of Satan*, will come to acknowledge that the Christians of Philadelphia are faithful and true believers according to the unlimited confidence which John of Patmos has in the power of Christ. John may well be thinking of the words of Isaiah 60:14, *The descendants of those who oppressed* *you shall come bending low to you, and all who despised you shall bow down at your feet.*

Criticism

There is none! The Christians of Philadelphia, like the Christians at Smyrna, suffer for their faith. Both groups are faithful and true. Therefore, they receive the unqualified praise of their Lord. They are encouraged to hold fast despite the opposition they face. Their Lord is near.

Conqueror

If you conquer, I will make you a pillar in the temple of my God; you will never go out of it. I will write on you the name of my God, and the name of the city of my God, the new Jerusalem that comes down from my God out of heaven, and my own new name. Let anyone who has an ear listen to what the Spirit is saying to the churches. (3:12-13)

The promise to every faithful believer includes two things.

First is being made *a pillar in the temple of my God*. In the Old Testament, there was a vision of a new temple in a new city after the exile of God's people. It is said, *As the glory of the LORD entered the temple by the gate facing east, the spirit lifted me up, and brought me into the inner court; and the glory of the LORD filled the temple. (Ezekiel 43:4-5)* As we shall see, Ezekiel's vision is fulfilled in John's dream of the future city with its unique temple! *And I saw the holy city, the new Jerusalem, coming down out of heaven from God ... I saw no temple in the city, for its temple is the Lord God the Almighty and the Lamb. (Revelation 21:2, 22)* To be made *a pillar in the temple of my God* is to dwell with God and so be made immune to the earthquakes of Philadelphia.

Second is being inscribed like a pillar with *the name of God and the name of the new Jerusalem and the new name* of the Son of God. It was also written of the new city in the Old Testament, *And the name of the city from that time on shall be, The LORD is There. (Ezekiel 48:35)* In Revelation 19:13, the new name is *The Word of God*. The conqueror who kept the name of Christ holy will be inscribed with the name of Christ. The citizens of Philadelphia knew that inscriptions on pillars in temples indicated the deities to whom the temples were dedicated. Similarly, the word picture of Christians being inscribed with the name of their Lord indicates that they belong to him in thought, word and deed.

Connections

When we see the doors that God opens for us, life and death take on new meaning and purpose. In life we find that we have opportunities to share the good news of Jesus. We find that God gives us openings to serve that we never dreamed of. In death we find that God provides a living hope and a heaven on earth destination. We find that there is a secure future for God's people.

7 The Throne of God

The letter to the church at Laodicea has as its key the idea of wholeheartedness. Christ gives a picture of a church in an affluent society and promises that repentance will open our lives to him who waits to enter and share life with us, as conquerors, individually and corporately.

> *To the one who conquers*
> *I will give a place with me on my throne,*
> *just as I myself conquered*
> *and sat down with my Father*
> *on his throne.*
> *(Revelation 3:21)*

Context

And to the angel of the church in Laodicea write. (3:14a)

Laodicea has been identified as a city of 'material prosperity, outward luxury, and physical health'. The city was sixty-four kilometres (forty miles) south east of Philadelphia. Laodicea was a banking centre, a manufacturer of black woollen cloth and a producer of eye ointment at its medical school. Whereas the cold water of Colossae refreshed the weary and the hot water of Hierapolis healed the sick, the lukewarm water of Laodicea was useless and harmful. After the earthquake of AD 60, Laodicea was too proud to accept imperial help for rebuilding. Laodicea, today, is a partly excavated ruin called Eski Hissar (meaning 'the old fortress') near Pamukkale (meaning 'white cotton'). Above modern Pamukkale with its gleaming white calcium cliffs and its springs of hot water are the ruins of ancient Hierapolis. Today, the ruins of Laodicea are south west of the excavations at Hierapolis and west of the mound of Colossae in the Lycus Valley.

Christ

The words of the Amen, the faithful and true witness, the origin of God's creation. (3:14b)

The description of Jesus is quite profound. He is God's Yes, *the Amen*, God's Revealer, *the faithful and true witness*, and Prime Source of God's Creation, *the origin of God's creation.*

Laodicea is only sixteen kilometres (ten miles) from Colossae. It is likely that the words of Paul's Letter to the Colossians were known by the Christians of Asia: *He is the image of the invisible God, the firstborn of all creation ... He is the head of the body, the church; he is the beginning, the firstborn from the dead, so that he might come to have first place in everything. (Colossians 1:15, 18)* Colossian and Laodicean Christians were challenged by Paul the Apostle and John the Seer to acknowledge the primacy of Christ over all.

Commendation

There is no commendation! Things were not as they seemed in Laodicea. In a city of people who are acknowledged as wealthy, healthy and well dressed, the believers of the city have nothing to commend them! The criticism that follows gives a devastating analysis of the church: *You do not realise that you are wretched, pitiable, poor, blind, and naked.*

Criticism

I know your works; you are neither cold nor hot. I wish that you were either cold or hot. So, because you are lukewarm, and neither cold nor hot, I am about to spit you out of my mouth. For you say, 'I am rich, I have prospered, and I need nothing.' You do not realise that you are wretched, pitiable, poor, blind, and naked. Therefore I counsel you to buy from me gold refined by fire so that you may be rich; and white robes to clothe you and to keep the shame of your nakedness from being seen; and salve to anoint your eyes so that you may see. I reprove and discipline those whom I love. Be earnest, therefore, and repent. (3:15-19)

The hot springs of Hierapolis are ten kilometres (six miles) from Laodicea. Below Hierapolis are white cliffs which are clearly visible from Laodicea. As the hot water makes its way to Laodicea, it loses its heat and becomes lukewarm, not therapeutically hot and not refreshingly cold. It is good for nothing. Indeed, Christ their Lord is pictured as vomiting the lukewarm Laodicean believers out of his mouth!

Despite their overflowing banks, the Laodicean Christians are poor; despite their physicians and medicines, they are sick and sightless; despite their clothing factories, they are naked. The Laodicean church has been adversely affected by the surrounding affluent society.

However, the Laodicean believers can become spiritually rich by being purified, *I counsel you to buy from me gold refined by fire so that you may be rich*, spiritually honoured by being put right, *white robes to clothe you and to keep the shame of your nakedness from being seen*, and spiritually perceptive by being enlightened, *salve to anoint your eyes so that you may see*. Christ's love issues in a general command, *Be earnest* (constantly), and a specific command, *Repent* (now).

Conqueror

Listen! I am standing at the door, knocking; if you hear my voice and open the door, I will come in to you and eat with you, and you with me. To the one who conquers I will give a place with me on my throne, just as I myself conquered and sat down with my Father on his throne. Let anyone who has an ear listen to what the Spirit is saying to the churches. (3:20-22)

As a friend Christ has admonished the Laodicean church to be earnest and to repent communally. Then as a friend Christ does more. He comes to the Laodicean Christians individually and seeks an entrance into each heart. Being earnest and being repentant opens life to the risen Lord who waits to enter and share life with believers communally and individually.

Amazingly, the Lord promises every faithful believer fellowship with him and with each other in his kingly rule. Christ shares the Father's throne because his victory is the Father's victory also, and the believer shares Christ's throne because his victory is Christ's too. The kingdom of God was inaugurated in the life of Jesus and will be consummated in his final victory. Meanwhile it is being realised in the followers of Jesus individually and communally.

Connections

Did the lukewarm believers in Laodicea have too many things going for them? Perhaps the Christians of Laodicea just let it all happen. They may have been saying, 'We just go with the flow and leave things up to the Holy Spirit!' Or they may have been saying, 'We're too busy keeping our activities going to stop and think about what we're really doing!' Or they may have been saying, 'We're on the cutting edge of ministering to the community and we can't pause to plan what actually happens!'

Challenges of the Seven Letters

James Blevins points out that the messages to the seven churches are not just lessons in history. The church down through the years has found comfort and help in the seven letters. Ephesus admonishes us to love God with our entire being. Smyrna reminds us of the need to persevere and overcome. Pergamum brings to mind the necessity to be aware of the dangers of false teachers. Thyatira gives us the opportunity to think of our faith in relation to our life-style. Sardis causes us to understand the need to be watchful and to do good works for Christ. Philadelphia stands as a symbol of an open door ministry available to the church of every era. Laodicea sets forth a picture of a self contented, lukewarm and spiritually impoverished church in the midst of material wealth.

BLESSINGS
in the Book of Revelation

Apocalypse Icon

Patmos Poster

8 The Reader and the Hearers

The reader faces a choice with his hearers. Seven blessings (Revelation 1:3; 14:13; 16:15; 19:9; 20:6; 22:7, 14) describe the way to honour and glory in the kingdom of God. Fourteen times (Revelation 8:13; 9:12; 11:14; 12:12; 18:10, 16, 19) the Greek word for 'woe' points to the righteous judgement of the creating and redeeming God upon unresponsive creatures who will not be redeemed. Will the reader and his hearers choose blessing or woe?

> *Blessed is the one who reads aloud*
> *the words of the prophecy,*
> *and blessed are those who hear*
> *and who keep what is written in it;*
> *for the time is near.*
> *(Revelation 1:3)*

Context

From the beginning to the end of the Revelation to John the one who reads and those who hear the drama of the book are encouraged to *keep what is written in it (1:3)* and to be *one who keeps the words of the prophecy of this book (22:7)*.

The book is a series of sevens accompanied by interludes. A vision of Christ who is the Son of Man promised in the Old Testament book of Daniel (Revelation 1:9-20) introduces letters to seven lampstands or churches in Asia Minor (Revelation 2:1 to 3:22). A vision of the control room at the heavenly headquarters (Revelation 4:1 to 5:14) leads to God's judgement by means of seals (Revelation 6:1-17; 8:1-5), trumpets (Revelation 8:6 to 9:21; 11:15-19), and bowls

(Revelation 15:1 to 16:21). Along the way there are three interludes: the Church Militant and Triumphant (Revelation 7:1-17), messages of assurance to John and his readers (Revelation 10:1 to 11:14), and good news to believers and bad news to unbelievers (Revelation 14:6-13). There are three further patterns of seven: seven sights (Revelation 12:1-14:5; 14:14-15:4), seven judgements (Revelation 17:1 to 20:3), and seven promises (Revelation 20:4 to 22:5).

As the drama unfolds reader and hearer are to exercise faith and obedience. This means letting the light of the last day, the ultimate victory of God, illumine the issues of the present day, the struggle between good and evil.

As biblical scholar Paul Minear said, John makes five assumptions. The reader will accept the divine presence as the basis of thought, word and deed. The reader is familiar with the story of Jesus the Lord. The reader is committed to rely on the divine power which shapes the future. The reader is willing to obey the orders of Christ, not Caesar. The reader is prepared to receive the prophet's message from the invisible God to the visible people of God.

If the reader ancient and modern can accept these assumptions, then he or she is on the way to rightly interpreting the drama with its series of sevens and accompanying interludes. It is hard work to unravel the book's threefold character of apocalyptic (akin to political and religious cartoons), prophecy (forthtelling of divine judgement and mercy), and epistle (letters to seven churches in the Roman Province of Asia). But it is worth it.

Content

Originally the book is circulated among the seven churches for reading aloud as it is received in public worship. There is one reader, *the one who reads aloud*, who is obviously literate and who can capture the dramatic nature of the book. There are also many illiterate hearers, *those who hear*, and who can benefit from a dramatic presentation of the book.

Reading allows for the reader's cross referencing of what else is written throughout the book. Hearing engages the hearers' association of whatever springs to the imagination individually and collectively. Whether it happens to be the reader or the listeners, they are all charged to pay attention to *the words of the prophecy*. Biblical prophecy is not foretelling but forthtelling. Reader and listeners are to *keep what is written* in the prophecy of John.

Reading and hearing implies that people learn to have faith in the God who speaks through the words of the book. Keeping implies that people learn to be obedient to the message which comes through the telling forth of God's judgement and mercy in the intriguing contents of the Revelation to John. As a result of faith and obedience, reader and listeners are *blessed*! Synonyms of *blessed* are fortunate, happy, privileged. Here the word relates to humans who are privileged recipients of God's favour.

All of this is because *the time is near.* John may be identifying what is already happening in the persecution of Christians at different times and places. This may foreshadow what is not yet happening but will happen at the end in the victory of God. With its theology of hope the book of Revelation is relevant in the times of crisis.

Connections

The late biblical scholar, F.F. Bruce, was a well known writer and therefore was asked to do lecture tours. His biographer, Tim Grass, tells two stories of him. They capture the spirit of the man very accurately.

He was a clear and coherent lecturer but somewhat stilted and dull. When he visited Australia in 1977, Bruce was invited to speak at St Andrew's Anglican Cathedral in Sydney. As he was being driven to the cathedral he saw a long line of people waiting to enter to hear the lecture. He said to his driver, 'My, these people will be disappointed.' Then he said to his host, 'And they were!' Bruce was not a good public speaker but he was a very good writer.

In England, Bruce was Rylands Professor of Biblical Criticism and Exegesis at the University of Manchester between 1959 and 1978. He was a faithful member at his church, a Brethren Assembly. A building site worker came to personal faith in Christ and joined the fellowship. His workmates asked him difficult questions about his new found faith and he would come back with clear and informative answers. After a while they asked him how he could give such good answers. 'There's an old fellow at our church called Fred. He seems to know all about these things.'

As a lecturer Bruce may have lacked vitality, but, as a follower of Jesus he was blessed because he read and wrote and lived what is written in the Bible.

Esther John

was a Pakistani convert who became a Presbyterian evangelist. She was killed probably by a Muslim fanatic in 1960.

Born Qamar Zia in 1929, she was strongly influenced by the teachers in a Madras Christian school at the age of seventeen. She came to Christian faith as she studied Isaiah 53. *'God put faith in my heart and I believed in Jesus as my Saviour and the forgiver of my sins.'*

After partition of India in 1947, her Muslim family moved to Karachi. Marian Laugesen gave her a New Testament to replace a Bible left behind in Madras. She read it secretly during the next seven years. Her parents tried to arrange a marriage with a Muslim but, in 1955, she ran away from home. She stayed in the homes of Marian Laugesan, who renamed her Esther John, and of an Anglican Bishop.

She moved further away and did a three year Bible course. She lived with American Presbyterian missionaries and became an evangelist on a bicycle. She was savagely killed on February 1, 1960. Her killer was never found. She was buried at Sahiwal, where a memorial chapel was later built. She had broken two taboos by living as a Christian and by refusing to marry a Muslim. Pakistan is still a perilous place to be a Christian convert.

9 The Faithful Dead

The new creation is not the reward, but there are rewards in the new heaven and the new earth.

> *And I heard a voice from heaven saying,*
> *"Write this:*
> *Blessed are the dead who from now on die in the Lord."*
> *"Yes," says the Spirit,*
> *"they will rest from their labours,*
> *for their deeds follow them."*
> *(Revelation 14:13)*

Context

The context of the second blessing is the drama of the Revelation to John as a whole. Throughout the book of Revelation we see and hear the blessing of the followers of Jesus as they march into the new heaven and the new earth to receive their rewards. We also see and hear the judging of the opponents of Jesus and his people.

Before the blessing there have been the opening of the Seven Seals of the scroll (The White Horse, The Red Horse, The Black Horse, The Pale Green Horse, The Martyrs, A Great Earthquake and Prayers of the Saints) and the sounding of the Seven Trumpets (Hail, Fire, Blood, Eruption of a Volcano, Pollution of Water, Darkness, Swarms of Locusts, War Horses and Coming of the Kingdom). After the blessing there will be the pouring of the Seven Bowls (Curse on the Earth, Curse on the Sea, Curse on the Rivers, Curse on the Sun, Curse on the Throne of the Beast, Curse on the Euphrates and Curse on the Air).

Content

In the midst of these judgements of God come negative and positive words. God's people are given (1) encouragement to faithfulness, *Here is a call for the endurance of the saints, those who keep the commandments of God and hold fast to their faith in Jesus*, and (2) assurance of eternal security, *Blessed are the dead who from now on die in the Lord ... they will rest from their labours, for their deeds follow them. (Revelation 14:12,13)*

John *heard a voice from heaven saying, 'Write this'*. This seems to parallel the opening vision of Christ when John *was in the spirit on the Lord's day* and *heard behind* him *a loud voice like a trumpet saying, 'Write in a book what you see and send it to the seven churches' (Revelation 1:10-11)*. Accordingly, if the parallel between Revelation 1:10-11 and 14:13 holds, the voice of Christ is commanding John to write, *Blessed are the dead who from now on die in the Lord.*

This blessing is aptly quoted at Christian funerals. *Blessed are the dead*. The blessed dead die *from now on*, from the time of the death and resurrection of Christ. They die *in the Lord*, in the sphere of Christ. Truly happy are all believers who die in the eternal now of Christ the Lord. They have remained faithful to Jesus until death.

The Spirit had affirmed the messages in the seven letters to the churches: *Let anyone who has an ear listen to what the Spirit is saying to the churches. (Revelation 2:7, 11, 17, 29; 3:6, 13, 22)*. The Spirit now responds to the blessing, *Blessed are the dead who from now on die in the Lord*, by saying, *Yes ... they will rest from their labours, for their deeds follow them*. At the end of the book the Spirit and the church will join in prayer to the Lord: *The Spirit and the bride say, 'Come.' (Revelation 22:17)*

The affirmation of the Spirit is twofold. First, the blessed dead *will rest from their labours*. The saints' everlasting rest will give respite from evil and death. Second, the *deeds* of the blessed dead *follow them*. Such good works are external signs of internal faith in Jesus. The words *labours* and *deeds* describe personal and communal faith actively expressed in everyday life.

Connections

A memorable example of someone who died in the Lord, who rested from his labours, and whose deeds followed him is an Italian who became known as God's minstrel, because he sang for God.

Francis of Assisi, 1181-1226, grew up as the favoured first son of a cloth merchant. He was a worldly twenty year old in stylish clothes when he became prisoner in a war between two Italian cities. His father purchased his freedom. But, in his mid-twenties Francis experienced gradual changes as he sought God's will. He gave generously to the poor, embraced lepers, sold his father's cloth and raised funds for the restoration of a chapel. His father enlisted the bishop of Assisi who tried unsuccessfully to dissuade Francis. Francis renounced his inheritance, took to repairing church buildings and wearing beggar's clothes. He desired to obey the command of Jesus to his disciples, *Take no gold, or silver, or copper in your belts, no bag for your journey, or two tunics, or sandals, or a staff; for labourers deserve their food. (Matthew 10:9-10)* He became a travelling preacher with a dozen disciples.

Francis travelled to North Africa in an attempt to convert Muslims to Christ. His life was marked by its simplicity of food, clothing and shelter. He reverenced working animals and domesticated birds. He cared for the sick, especially lepers. Francis was said to have healed the gravely ill and to have tamed the wild animals. He preached to the birds! In his travels he preached to the Muslim Sultan in Egypt. He emphasised the practice of the Eucharist or Communion. He popularised the celebration of Christmas with a nativity scene including shepherds with sheep, cattle around the manger, Joseph and Mary with donkey, wise men with camels, and, of course, the Baby Jesus ... altogether in the one place at the one time! Towards the end of his life Francis received on his body the stigmata, the marks of the Crucified.

Although he instructed his followers to be 'poor in goods, but exalted in virtues', later Franciscans struggled to live up to his ideal. Eventually there were three orders of Franciscans: the Friars Minor (males), the Poor Clares (females), and the Penitents (lay men and women). The spirit of Francis is captured in 'The Canticle of the Sun', an authentic writing of his in 1225. (On the other hand, 'The Prayer of St Francis' first appeared in a 1912 French publication and was translated into English in 1927.) Francis was canonised by the Roman Church two years after his death. Truly, Francis died in the Lord, rested from his labours, and his deeds followed him.

A group of Franciscans who sought to return to the original ideals of Francis in the 1520s wore coarse robes with a distinctive hood (cappuccio) and became known as Capuchins. Ironically, they are remembered for their special brew of coffee, the cappuccino!

Martin Luther King

was an African-American Baptist minister who campaigned for civil rights. He was assassinated in 1968.

King, born in Atlanta in 1929, was the grandson and son of African-American Baptist pastors. He attended segregated public schools and an African-American college in Atlanta before he studied in the north at Crozier Theological Seminary and Boston University.

In 1954 Martin returned to the south as a Baptist pastor. At personal risk, he participated in the Montgomery bus boycott in 1956 which, despite white violence, led to integration of the buses. He became president of the Southern Christian Leadership Conference.

Influenced by the Sermon on the Mount and the non-violent technique of Gandhi, King campaigned for civil rights and sought to teach white people how to love their black brothers and sisters.

In 1963 he wrote his *'Letter from a Birmingham Jail'*. That year he delivered his famous *'I have a dream'* speech to 250,000 people in Washington. In 1967 he was awarded the Nobel Peace Prize.

On April 4, 1968 Martin Luther King was assassinated in Memphis. The night before he died he said to his followers, *'I may not get there with you, but I want you to know that we as a people will get to the promised land.'*

10 The Sentinel

John is warning his readers that, just as the last days of Rome would come suddenly, so would the coming of Christ also be like a thief in the night.

> *"See, I am coming like a thief!*
> *Blessed is the one who stays awake*
> *and is clothed,*
> *not going about naked*
> *and exposed to shame."*
> *(Revelation 16:15)*

Context

The Revelation to John portrays the judgements of God in a series of seven seals of a scroll being opened, seven trumpets being sounded and seven bowls being poured out. Towards the end of the seven bowls the third blessing interrupts the drama of curses on earth, sea, rivers, the Beast's throne, the River Euphrates and the air.

After it is said that foul spirits like frogs gather the kings of the world for battle on the great day of God the Almighty (Revelation 16:14), and before it is said that the place of assembly is Armageddon (Revelation 16:16), the voice of the heavenly Christ announces his unexpected coming with the third blessing.

Because it is an interruption, some scholars have suggested that Revelation 16:15 is inappropriate in its present location. Indeed, two commentators believe that the verse belongs at Revelation 3:3. Such scholars were inclined to rewrite

Revelation if they thought it did not agree with their theories of differing sources or underlying forms. In fact, the warning is appropriate as it stands between the great day of God the Almighty and the place called Armageddon (Revelation 16:14, 16). The victory of good over evil is described in the vivid symbolism of Revelation 19:17-21 and 20:7-10.

Content

It has been said that John writes in Greek but thinks in Hebrew! Indeed, the flavour of the Greek version of the Hebrew Old Testament influences the book of Revelation so that the medium becomes the message. The author of Revelation has a quirky way with the Greek language and is indebted to Biblical Greek. For example, *See*, is traditionally translated 'Behold'. It appears in the Greek version of the Old Testament and is often used in the New Testament. It prompts readers and hearers to pay attention.

Like an Old Testament prophet, John brings the words of the Lord in this third blessing to readers and hearers of his dramatic book: *I am coming like a thief!* John is in noble company as he delivers the words of Jesus the Lord. Jesus himself had warned his disciples: *But understand this: if the owner of the house had known in what part of the night the thief was coming, he would have stayed awake and would not have let his house be broken into. Therefore you also must be ready, for the Son of Man is coming at an unexpected hour. (Matthew 24:43-44)* Paul also had warned his readers: *you yourselves know very well that the day of the Lord will come like a thief in the night. (1 Thessalonians 5:2)*

John had written to the church of Sardis, *If you do not wake up, I will come like a thief, and you will not know at what hour I will come to you. (Revelation 3:3)* Now he writes, *See, I am coming like a thief! (Revelation 16:15a)* Both warnings are to be taken seriously. The readers and hearers of the Revelation to John are sentinels who sometimes forget the fight between good and evil in which they are engaged.

This is the third *Blessed* of Revelation (1:3; 14:13; 16:15; 19:9; 20:6; 22:7, 14). The reader and listeners are fortunate, happy and privileged recipients of God's favour. They are to be as *the one who stays awake and is clothed, not going about naked and exposed to shame.* They are to be aware and prepared, not unaware and unprepared, for the coming judgement.

The word pictures parallel references made in letters to two of the seven churches. One had received the assessment, *You have still a few persons in Sardis who have not soiled their clothes; they will walk with me, dressed in white, for they are worthy. If you conquer, you will be clothed like them in white robes. (Revelation 3:4-5)* The other had been advised, *I counsel you to buy from me ... white robes to clothe you and to keep the shame of your nakedness from being seen. (Revelation 3:18)*

The original audience of John's dramatic message would be conscious that Jesus who says, *I am coming like a thief!* has won the victory on the cross. As the new song in John's vision of heaven says, *You were slaughtered and by your blood you ransomed for God saints from every tribe and language and people and nation; you have made them to be a kingdom and priests serving our God, and they will reign on earth. (Revelation 5:9-10)*

The kingdom of God has already come and Jesus has won the decisive victory in his birth and life, death and resurrection. However, the kingdom of God is still to come in the fullness of time and God will bring everything into a unity in Christ. In the meantime, the followers of Jesus are engaged in an ongoing struggle in which the victory is assured.

Connections

The readers and hearers of the Revelation to John are meant to be sentinels who are mindful of the fight between good and evil in which they are engaged. These sentinels know the difference between disgrace and grace.

A contemporary example is Hoa Van Stone. He was born about 1966 and was taken in by an orphanage in Saigon, South Vietnam, two years later. He suffered polio as a child and this resulted in a life long disability. In 1975, at the close of the war in Vietnam, he was part of Operation Babylift and finished up in Adelaide, South Australia. Eventually he was fostered and then adopted by a Christian couple, Brian and Kathleen Stone.

Along the way there were times of joy and sorrow. Hoa experienced the wonder of becoming part of a family with other children. He went through profound grief because of the death of one of those children. He remembers the encouragement of his parents, the challenges of his schooling, the corrective surgery of his adolescence, the pressure of his high school peer group, and the outbreak of rebellion at the age of sixteen.

The sad and sorry story includes leaving home, drifting into drug dependency and becoming involved in dealing in drugs. The unexpected happened when he prayed in despair for God's help and discovered that he had lost the desire for heroin and cannabis. Moving out of the drug world, Hoa was reconciled with his parents as he learned to live as a Christian. He also made the decision to give up things that were addictive such as tobacco and alcohol.

Hoa was indebted to a returned missionary who took him on as a boarder and to the Burleigh College staff and students who helped him study with a view to future service. He developed the habit of writing a journal recording the ups and downs of life as a follower of Jesus. In time he became pastor of a Sydney Vietnamese church and was finally recognised by the Baptists of Adelaide through ordination in 1997.

Hoa's story continued with his return to Saigon, now known as Ho Chi Minh City, in Vietnam. There he relearnt his native language. There he has been the agent of helping children and young persons with a physical disability to find a brighter future. This is occurring through the Company of Grace with a dedicated band of workers to equip people and develop their skills. Thereby disabled young persons are being enabled to enjoy a useful and whole life.

We cannot but be moved by what a man with a crippled body has gone through, by his faith in God who has given him a second chance, and by his conviction that all of life's experiences can be put to good use as we seek to be followers of Jesus. It is still true that as we read or hear Revelation we can learn to be sentinels on behalf of Jesus who has won in the fight between good and evil.

Wang Zhiming

was a Chinese pastor and evangelist. He was executed during the Cultural Revolution by the Red Guards in 1973.

Wang was born in 1907 of Miao nationality in Yunnan province a year after the China Inland Mission came to Wuding county with words and deeds that transformed lives.

After the Communist Revolution in 1949 Wang was a recognised Christian leader in place of expelled missionaries. Between 1951 and 1953 he refused to participate in accusation meetings to denounce landlords and American imperialists. As a delegate to Beijing Wang met Chairman Mao in 1956.

By 1958 religion in Yunnan was being attacked by the authorities. Wang was jailed in 1969. Before his cruel execution at a rally of 10,000 in 1973 he said to some family members, *'You should follow the words from above, and repent once again.'* The work of the Red Guards was overturned in 1976. In 1980 Wang's name was rehabilitated.

Today around 30,000 Christians in more than 100 churches of Wuding remember Wang. Near his home is the only known monument to a Christian martyr of the Cultural Revolution. Its inscription includes the words, *As Scripture says of the Saints, 'They will rest from their labours for their deeds follow them'*.

11 The Guests

Three biblical pictures of the church as the people of God, the body of Christ and the fellowship of the Spirit will find their fulfilment when Jesus is revealed in glory and his followers are invited by him to share his joy.

> *And the angel said to me,*
> *"Write this:*
> *Blessed are those who are invited*
> *to the marriage supper of the Lamb."*
> *And he said to me,*
> *"These are true words of God."*
> *(Revelation 19:9)*

Context

The fourth blessing recapitulates the theme of an earlier scene: *The kingdom of the world has become the kingdom of our Lord and of his Messiah, and he will reign forever and ever. (Revelation 11:15)* Human society, which is temporarily organised in opposition to God, must eventually become subject to its creator and redeemer.

An angelic being gives the fourth blessing during a series of seven judgements of God portrayed in Revelation 17:1 to 20:3. The dramatic narrative records the judgement of the Great Whore in apocalyptic imagery, the fall of the Great City in a prophetic dirge, the marriage of the Lamb in heavenly praise, the victory of the Word of God in company with the armies of heaven, the summons of an angel in the sun, the defeat of the Beast and the False Prophet, and the imprisonment of the Devil who is the accuser or slanderer of humans.

In the midst of such sombre descriptions of sorrowful judgement comes the good news that the church is united with its Lord and shares the joy of his kingdom when he is revealed in divine glory. John is told to write this blessing in no uncertain terms. It is in direct contrast to its context of judgement.

Content

The angel who says the fourth blessing to John is probably the mighty angel who casts a great stone into the sea and says that *Babylon the great city* will suffer a similar fate due to its maltreatment of *prophets* and *saints* in Revelation 18:21-24. This angel refuses the worship of John and identifies himself as *a fellow servant* in Revelation 19:10.

Three times in Revelation 19:9-10 John records that the angel *said to me*. Literally, the Greek is the historic present, 'he says to me'. John senses the immediate presence of the angelic being as he receives the command, *Write this*.

John has transmitted previous blessings to the reader and hearers (Revelation 1:3), to the faithful dead who rest in the Lord (Revelation 14:13), to the believer who acts as a sentinel of the coming king (Revelation 16:15). Now he conveys a blessing to believers who are invited to and who wait for the future heavenly banquet (Revelation 19:9).

There is a double symbolism relating to the idea of an elaborate celebratory dinner for the Messiah. In verse 7 it is said that the Lamb's followers are *his bride*. In verse 9 it is said that the Lamb's followers are guests at *the marriage supper of the Lamb*.

There are Old Testament images of Israel as the bride of the Lord. For example, God says, *I will take you for my wife forever; I will take you for my wife in righteousness and in justice, in steadfast love, and in mercy. I will take you for my wife in faithfulness; and you shall know the LORD. (Hosea 2:19-20)*

There are also New Testament images of the church as the bride of Christ: *Christ loved the church and gave himself up for her, in order to make her holy by cleansing her with the washing of water by the word, so as to present the church to himself in splendor, without a spot or wrinkle or anything of the kind — yes, so that she may be holy and without blemish. (Ephesians 5:25-27)*

Furthermore, there are Old Testament references to a great feast for the world. For instance, in 'the apocalypse of Isaiah' there is a promise to Jerusalem, *On this mountain the LORD of hosts will make for all peoples a feast of rich food, a feast of well-aged wines... (Isaiah 25:6)*

Likewise, there are New Testament references to a grand banquet for God's people. Jesus tells two parables: one about a wedding feast for a son (Matthew 22:1-14) and another about a great dinner for friends (Luke 14:15-24).

It may be that verse 7 is a corporate picture of the church who is about to be married to the Lamb and that verse 9 is an individual picture of believers who are invited as guests to the marriage banquet of the Lamb.

At this stage it is worth referring to Revelation 4 and 5. Just as the creating God was accounted *worthy* of worship and receives *glory and honour and power* in Revelation 4, the redeeming Lamb in Revelation 5 is accounted *worthy* of worship and receives *glory and honour and power*. The worship offered to God the Lord is to the Creator who has plans for his creation and the worship offered to Christ the Lamb is to the Redeemer who accomplishes the plans of his Father.

In the light of this, we return to Revelation 19. *And the angel said to me, "Write this: Blessed are those who are invited to the marriage supper of the Lamb." And he said to me, "These are true words of God."* The fourth blessing which expresses divine truth in verse 9 leads to a dialogue between John the seer and the angelic being in verse 10. *Then I fell down at his feet to worship him, but he said to me, "You must not do that! I am a fellow servant with you and your comrades who hold the testimony of Jesus. Worship God! For the testimony of Jesus is the spirit of prophecy."* Not the angel but the God and Father of our Lord Jesus Christ is the rightful object of worship. Do not mistake the messenger for the Message! Do not confuse the creation with the Creator!

This is in accord with the overall message of the Revelation to John. The True Trinity (the Lord, the Lamb, the Spirit) defeats the false trinity (the Beast, the False Prophet, the Devil). One thinks of the words of John the elder, *We are in him who is true, in his Son Jesus Christ. He is the true God and eternal life. Little children, keep yourselves from idols. (1 John 5:20-21)*

Connections

As we have noted, the word pictures of a bride and a wedding banquet suggest the celebration of the coming of the kingdom of God. It is helpful to describe the original concepts surrounding the kingdom of God.

The Gospels see God's kingly activity in Jesus. He rescues people from sin and evil. He commences a new godly community with a new style of living. His people share his sufferings and know his resurrection power. His people look forward to Jesus' final victory.

Sometimes people in a world with few kings and queens find it useful to think of the divine dominion in other ways. Following the suggestions of Brian McLaren, a thought provoking author, we may explore several metaphors which can bring fresh meaning to the New Testament's message about God's kingdom.

First, the dream of God for creation may appeal to parents who have great dreams for their children or artists who have unique dreams for the products of their artistry.

Second, the revolutionary movement of God may suggest a move from war to peace, from the material to the spiritual, from hate to love, from enmity to reconciliation, from injustice to justice.

Third, the healing mission of God may call to mind that believers are healed of the viral infection of evil and death so that they can join in bringing God's well being of goodness and life to others.

Fourth, the party of God may suggest the holding of a street party to which everyone in the neighbourhood is invited and which is a celebration of faith in Christ, hope for the future, and God's love.

Fifth, the network of God may appeal to the information technology experts who can envisage communication to and from God and interconnectedness with believers through a worldwide web.

Finally, the dance of God may call to mind an early church idea of the Trinity, the mutual indwelling of Father, Son, and Spirit in a harmonious dance. People who have forsaken the dance of God are being invited to rejoin it through Jesus, the Lord of the Dance.

Whichever metaphor we find most helpful we are seeking to be followers of Jesus in whom we see God at work, rescuing us from sin and evil, incorporating us into a new godly community with a new style of living, sharing the sufferings of Jesus, knowing the power of his resurrection and looking forward to his final victory.

Janani Luwum

was Anglican Archbishop of Uganda. He was killed by order of Idi Amin in 1977.

Born in 1922, Luwum was dramatically converted in 1948 and said, *'Today I have become a leader in Christ's army. I am prepared to die in the army of Jesus. As Jesus shed his blood for the people, if it is God's will, I will do the same.'* The school teacher turned evangelist, then studied for the Anglican ministry.

He became Bishop of Northern Uganda in 1969 and Archbishop of Uganda in 1974.

Janani confronted internal disharmony in the church and external persecution from the state. He used a hunting analogy, *'The best way to show a stick that is crooked is not to argue about it or to spend time denouncing it, but to lay a straight stick alongside it.'*

At great risk, Luwum spoke personally with Idi Amin, a Muslim, about his regime's injustice when his opponents were murdered or expelled.

After he handed a note of protest to Idi Amin, Janani was accused of treason, was arrested with two Christian cabinet ministers, and the three were shot dead on February 16, 1977. His body was never found. Amin was deposed in 1979.

12 The Holy and Hopeful

Reinhold Niebuhr in *The Nature and Destiny of Man* (1943) gave a memorable warning: 'It is unwise for Christians to claim any knowledge of either the furniture of heaven or the temperature of hell, or to be too certain about any details of the Kingdom of God in which history is consummated.'

> *Blessed and holy are those who share*
> *in the first resurrection.*
> *Over these the second death has no power,*
> *but they will be priests of God and of Christ,*
> *and they will reign with him a thousand years.*
> *(Revelation 20:6)*

Context

The fifth blessing is given at the beginning of seven promises: the thousand years, the judgement of evil, a new heaven and a new earth, their God and my children, the holy city, the light of the city and the river of life (Revelation 20:4 to 22:5).

These seven promises are a dramatic outworking of the big picture of the Bible story, including the vision of Daniel, the prayer of Jesus and the hope of Paul.

> Daniel dreamed of *one like a human being coming with the clouds of heaven. And he came to the Ancient One and was presented before him. To him was given dominion and glory and kingship, that all peoples, nations, and languages should serve him. His dominion is an everlasting dominion that shall not pass away, and*

his kingship is one that shall never be destroyed. (Daniel 7:13-14)

Jesus prayed, *Your kingdom come. Your will be done, on earth as it is in heaven. (Matthew 6:10)*

Paul hoped for *the end, when he (Christ) hands over the kingdom to God the Father, after he has destroyed every ruler and every authority and power. For he must reign until he has put all his enemies under his feet. The last enemy to be destroyed is death. (1 Corinthians 15:24-26)*

At the beginning of the seven promises comes the intriguing and mysterious blessing involving a thousand years reign of Christ and his followers.

Content

First, we note a particular grammatical feature.

The phrase *blessed and holy* is literally singular in the original Greek. The NRSV translates the phrase as plural - *Blessed and holy are those who share in the first resurrection* - probably because it seeks to be inclusive of men and women. The following words are translated in the plural - *Over these the second death has no power, but they will be priests of God and of Christ, and they will reign with him a thousand years* - in accord with the original Greek.

Second, we seek to spell out the meaning of various concepts.

Blessed is once again used to indicate a person who is privileged to receive God's steadfast love. *Holy* is added to describe such a person as consecrated to God's service in purity and reverence.

The first resurrection is a phrase unique to John the seer. First, it has been explained as the first of two physical resurrections, one of the martyrs who died for their testimony to Jesus, the other of all of God's people. Second, it has been explained as the entry of all of God's people into an intermediate state after death before the resurrection at the end of time. Third, it has been explained as an anticipated resurrection symbolised in baptism of the believer with a view to the general resurrection still to come.

The second death is a spiritual death which takes place after physical death. It is the fate of those who reject God's kind of life in a new heaven and a new earth. Spiritual death is described in ghastly symbolism: *This is the second death, the lake of fire.(Revelation 20:14)* It is a reality which is beyond words.

Priests of God and of Christ who *will reign with him* (that is, God and Christ!) *a thousand years* is a description of the followers of Jesus with affinities to words of the four living creatures and the twenty-four elders: *you have made them to be a kingdom and priests serving our God, and they will reign on earth. (Revelation 5:10)* The followers of Jesus share his royal authority over the whole creation and his priestly work in the worldwide mission and ministry of the church.

The temporal phrase, *a thousand years*, has been much debated. The Latin word for 'a thousand' is *mille*. Hence *a thousand years* is called a millenium.

Briefly, there have been three interpretations of the millenium, the thousand years, in Revelation 20.

First, the nineteenth century was the great era of Christian missionary endeavour and Christian social reform. It was seen by some as a time merging into the millenium of goodness and light. Christ's second coming was expected at the end of the millenium. This is the optimistic **postmillenial** view. The world would get better and better. Progress would be evident in missionary expansion and social change.

Second, the late nineteenth century until the late twentieth century was a period in which there was a rebirth of a second century phenomenon. The Greek word for 'a thousand' is *chilia*. Thus belief in a literal thousand year reign of Christ was called chiliasm. The church of the second century was slow to accept the Book of Revelation because of its apparent chiliasm. Eventually, the church accepted the Book of Revelation but rejected literalistic chiliasm or millenarianism.

However, in the late eighteenth century there was a resurgence of millenarianism in the form of premillennialism. Christ's second coming was expected before the millenium. This is the pessimistic **premillenial** view. The world would get worse and worse. Signs of the times would lead to a complicated timetable of doom and gloom before the millenium and then the final judgement.

Third, between the fourth and nineteenth centuries the dominant interpretation of the millenium was symbolic. A thousand is based on ten which, in the number code of apocalyptic, means completeness. Since his death and resurrection Christ has been reigning spiritually until the end of the age. This is the spiritual **amillenial** view with no future thousand year reign. Meanwhile the struggle between good and evil continues, although the decisive victory has been won by Christ crucified and risen.

In conclusion, it is worth noting that the Bible only mentions a thousand years reign in Revelation 20:2-7. In a book full of symbols it seems perilous to seek chronological exactitude at the expense of theological truth in interpreting the millenium of Revelation 20. The people of God come to life with Christ crucified and risen, serve as priests with Christ in the worldwide church, and rule as kings with Christ over the whole creation.

As James Blevins says, we don't have enough conclusive evidence to write an exclusively postmillenial or premillenial or amillenial theology. It may be that the best option is to agree with the country preacher who said, 'I am a Panmillenialist; it is all going to pan out in the end anyway, why worry about it?'

Connections

According to the fifth blessing the readers and hearers of the Revelation to John are meant to be priests and kings. They represent God and Christ as priests and they reign with Christ as kings.

A most unlikely example is a seventeen year old who served on an anti-aircraft battery during the fire bombing of Hamburg in July 1943. The German youth survived. His nearby friend was torn apart. Everybody looked at the survivor as a miracle. For the first time in his life he cried out for God. His name was Jürgen Moltmann.

A year later Jürgen was called up for military training and then was a reluctant member of the infantry forces. After six months in the German army he became a relieved but depressed prisoner of war, in February 1945. Eventually he was shipped to Scotland where he worked as a manual labourer and then as an interpreter. The friendship of the Scots with whom he worked was a blessing.

In time Jürgen became aware of the evil of the Nazi concentration camps and his patriotic feelings fell away. Two things saved him from utter despair. First, there was the humanity of the Scots who accepted him. Second, there was an army chaplain's gift of a Bible. Jürgen read it in the evenings and it came alive to him when he read the Psalms of lament.

Then Jürgen went on to read the whole of Mark's Gospel and came to the cry of Jesus on the cross: *My God, my God, why have you forsaken me? (Mark 15:34)* He began to understand Jesus because in Jürgen's mind, Jesus understood him. Jesus became 'the divine brother in need, the companion on the way, who goes with you through this "valley of the shadow of death", the fellow-sufferer who carries you, with your suffering.' Jürgen slowly but surely found assurance of the companionship of Christ.

This was the beginning of Jürgen's life as a follower of Jesus. He was to become a theology student, then a pastor, then a seminary professor, and eventually a renowned author. He published such memorable books as *The Theology of Hope*, *The Crucified God*, *The Church in the Power of the Spirit*, *God in Creation*, and *The Coming of God*. Jürgen Moltmann never forgot his indebtedness to the portrayal of Jesus in Mark's Gospel. In terms of the fifth blessing of Revelation, he learned to be a fellow traveller with all who represent God and Christ as priests and reign with Christ as kings.

Oscar Romero

was Roman Catholic Archbishop of San Salvador, who was an advocate for social justice. He was assassinated in 1980.

Born in 1917 and ordained in 1942, Romero became an auxiliary bishop in 1970, then a rural bishop in 1974, and an archbishop in 1977. His conservatism was challenged by the government sanctioned killing of a Jesuit friend a month after Oscar became archbishop. He revealed an openness to the poor and a defence of human rights.

Oscar was criticised by bishops, misunderstood by the Pope, opposed by the government, threatened by the military, attacked by the media and ignored by the US. Meanwhile people were 'disappearing' due to government sponsored repression. Romero's broadcast and published sermons threw the light of the Gospel on the suffering of the Salvadoran people.

In early March 1980 he said, *'I must tell you, as a Christian, I do not believe in death without resurrection. If I am killed, I shall arise in the Salvadoran people ... If the threats are carried out, from this moment I offer my blood to God for the redemption and for the resurrection of El Salvador ... You may say, if they succeed in killing me, that I pardon and bless those who do it ... A bishop will die, but God's church, which is the people, will never perish.'* On March 24, 1980 Oscar was gunned down as he led mass in the chapel of the hospital where he lived.

13 The Obedient

The end is not a sequence of events leading to a final event, but the one and only person who is from first to last, from start to finish.

"See, I am coming soon!
Blessed is the one
who keeps the words
of the prophecy of this book."
(Revelation 22:7)

Context

The sixth blessing occurs after the judgement of all that is evil and after the salvation of heaven and earth. On the one hand, the devil, the beast and the false prophet are condemned. Death and Hades are given over to the second death with anyone whose name is not in the book of life. On the other hand, in the new heaven and the new earth the conquerors experience their relationship with God as his children. The holy city has the glory of God as its light. The river of life flows through its midst as God's servants worship the Lord and the Lamb.

The sixth blessing is at the beginning of the conclusion of the Revelation to John. There are interesting parallels between the introduction and the conclusion of the book. In both, the book is described as genuine prophecy, the words are to be read in churches, and the reader and the hearers are encouraged to be faithful and true to the Lord and the Lamb.

These similarities point to the consistent message throughout the book. Salvation awaits those who practise the truth proclaimed by John the prophet and judgement is the fate of those who practise the falsehood typified by the powers of evil and death.

Content

Beforehand, the angel tells John that his words are trustworthy and true, because the God of true prophets had sent him to reveal the reality of God's purpose for his people and his world (Revelation 22:6).

Then Christ gives the sixth blessing to John.

As we have noted previously, *See* or 'Behold!' appears in the Greek version of the Old Testament and is often used in the New Testament. It prompts reader or hearer to pay attention.

The promise, *I am coming soon*, can be understood as an assurance that the final victory of Christ will come in God's good time. Although readers and hearers are not told the exact date or hour, they are to be prepared.

Meanwhile, the obedient reader or hearer is called *blessed*. That is to say, as we also noted previously, such a person is privileged to receive God's steadfast love.

Obedience means being *one who keeps the words of the prophecy* in *this book*. As prophecy the Revelation to John is in the tradition of Old Testament prophets who announced the judgement and mercy of God in the midst of the struggle between good and evil.

Ben Witherington has paraphrased the sixth blessing: 'Blessing comes to those who live by the words of this book.'

Afterward, John responds by falling down to worship the angel and is reproved by the angel who tells him to worship not the creature but the God who creates, reveals and redeems (Revelation 22:8-9).

Connections

The readers and hearers of the Revelation to John are encouraged to be people who seek to trust and obey the God who is both Creator and Redeemer. It is a case of being his people and doing his purpose.

Francis Collins has gained fame as head of the Human Genome Project. He works as a scientist in the study of DNA, the code of life. Unlike some notorious atheists who are scientists, Collins is in favour of God and science. He tells his story in an absorbing book entitled *The Language of God*.

Collins grew up in a family who appreciated church music but not Christian faith. After high school he went to university in Virginia where he became an agnostic. He simply did not know if God existed or not. Indeed, he didn't want to know.

When he advanced to a Ph.D. programme in chemistry at Yale, he then moved from agnosticism to atheism. He did not believe that God existed. However, he left his study of chemistry for medical school in North Carolina. During his third year of medicine he was challenged by a dying Christian patient who asked what he believed. Francis began to investigate the major world religions to bolster his atheism.

He was confused and visited a nearby Methodist minister to make enquiries. After hearing him out, the minister gave him a book to read. It was *Mere Christianity* by C.S. Lewis. In time, the books of C.S. Lewis opened the mind of Francis to other possibilities. Belief appeared more reasonable than unbelief. He sensed a 'God-shaped vacuum' in his life.

Soon Francis came to the point of believing in some sort of God. Then a year later he felt that he was being called to account. During autumn he was hiking in the Cascade Mountains and was struck by the beauty of a frozen waterfall. The splendour of God's creation overwhelmed him. As he describes his experience of the next day, 'I knelt in the dewy grass as the sun rose and surrendered to Jesus Christ.'

Francis Collins had become one with the people who seek to trust and obey God in Christ who is both Creator and Redeemer, *the Alpha and the Omega, the first and the last, the beginning and the end. (Revelation 22:12)*

14 The Cleansed

H. Richard Niebuhr in *The Kingdom of God in America* (1937) summarised and critiqued a sentimental version of the message of Jesus which spoke of 'a God without wrath' who 'brought men' and women 'without sin into a Kingdom without judgement through the ministrations of a Christ without a Cross.'

> ***Blessed are those who wash their robes,***
> ***so that they will have the right to the tree of life***
> ***and may enter the city by the gates.***
> ***(Revelation 22:14)***

Context

First, the book's conclusion emphasises the authenticity of its message of divine revelation. John the seer *heard and saw these things* and the angel calls him *a fellow servant* and numbers him among *the prophets*; the angel was sent by Jesus the Lord *with this testimony for the churches*; and the hearers are warned neither to add to nor to take away *words of the prophecy of this book. (Revelation 22:8-9, 16, 18-19)*

Second, the book's conclusion also stresses the nearness of the fulfilment of its message. Jesus says, *I am coming soon*; the angel says that *the time is near*; he repeats, *I am coming soon*; and he reaffirms, *Surely I am coming soon. (Revelation 22:7, 10, 12, 20)*

Thus the long and winding road of the seven blessings reaches its end. Half way through the conclusion of the book of Revelation comes the seventh blessing. The reader or hearer faces a choice between seven blessings (Revelation 1:3; 14:13; 16:15; 19:9; 20:6; 22:7, 14) and fourteen woes (Revelation 8:13; 9:12; 11:14; 12:12; 18:10, 16, 19). Do we choose the way to honour and glory inside the holy city or the way to impiety and immorality outside the holy city?

Content

The seventh blessing is a positive statement about those over whom spiritual death, mentioned in Revelation 20:6, 14, has no power. The favour of God rests upon the *blessed*, because they *wash their robes*, because they *will have the right to the tree of life*, and because they *may enter the city by the gates*.

Washing robes recalls Revelation 7:14 and 12:11. The former describes the purified, persevering, protected followers of Jesus whose atoning death has transformed their lives. *These are they who have come out of the great ordeal; they have washed their robes and made them white in the blood of the Lamb.* The latter portrays the believers who benefit from the triumph of the Lamb of God on the cross and who testify to the defeat of evil and death in the crucified and risen Christ. *They have conquered him* (Satan, the accuser) *by the blood of the Lamb and by the word of their testimony.*

The Bible story starts with the garden of Eden in Genesis 2 and ends with the holy city, the new Jerusalem, in Revelation 21. Features of a garden exist in the city, namely, *the river of the water of life* and *the tree of life. (Revelation 22:1, 2)* As we saw in the letter to Ephesus in Revelation 2:7, *the tree of life* had three associations: the contrast between paradise lost in Genesis 2 and paradise regained in Revelation 22; the tree at the centre of the temple of Artemis as a place of asylum for unrepentant criminals; and the death of Jesus on a tree as a place of refuge for repentant sinners. Eating fruit from *the tree of life* is to experience God's kind of life.

Entering the holy city is opposite to staying outside the holy city. Revelation 22:14 deals with those who wish to be inside the holy city. They have taken responsibility to *wash their robes* and have received the privilege to *enter the city by the gates*. It is likely that the twelve gates of the city symbolise the members of the new Israel with the twelve apostles of the Lamb (Revelation 21:12-14).

But, according to Revelation 22:15, there are those who choose to be outside the holy city: *the dogs and sorcerers and fornicators and murderers and idolaters, and everyone who loves and practices falsehood.* It is likely that *the dogs* is a metaphor for the morally unclean. Revelation 21:8 has a similar list: *the cowardly, the faithless, the polluted, the murderers, the fornicators, the sorcerers, the idolaters, and all liars.*

Connections

Two gifts which help us experience being redeemed by the atoning death of Christ and being recipients of the grace of God are encouragement and assurance. The autobiography of Glenn Hinson provides illustrations of both gifts. Hinson came from very humble origins to distinguished academic positions. However, without encouragement and assurance he would never have attained the stature of a biblical scholar, a church historian and a spiritual guide.

Encouragement came his way in the person of a young teacher at a small Missouri one teacher primary school. When Glenn's world was falling apart during the separation and divorce of his parents during his second grade, Bertha Brown would put her hand on his shoulder and say, 'You can make it, Glenn. You can make it.' Glenn knew that he could because this woman in her twenties was always there to teach eight grades of children reading, writing and arithmetic. When she died of cancer thirty-five years later she showed the same spirit. She told Glenn, 'I'll make it, whatever comes.'

Assurance was also given to Glenn when he was a third year university student and was seeking a relevant faith. One morning he woke up at two o'clock and felt a powerful presence. The words of Jesus in John 8:32 burned in his consciousness, 'You will know the truth, and the truth will make you free.' Glenn realised the personal nature of the truth and experienced the freedom to live his life in relationship with God. He has never had to look backwards from that decision. He came to identify with Blaise Pascal and Soren Kierkegaard. He made it his aim to do his best with who he was and what he had.

Along with many other students, I am glad that Glenn Hinson received the gifts of encouragement and assurance. He passed them on to his students in biblical studies, church history and contemplative spirituality. As celebrated author Frederick Buechner has said, it is not so much their subjects that great teachers teach as it is themselves. That was certainly true of Glenn Hinson.

PERPLEXING QUESTIONS & INTRIGUING ANSWERS

Who are the angels of the seven churches?

The seven stars are the angels of the seven churches, and the seven lampstands are the seven churches. (Revelation 1:20)

1 Heavenly guardians of the churches: Guardian angels are responsible for the welfare of each congregation. Could a human writer have been instructed to write the words of Christ to supernatural beings? Could angels have been held guilty of their churches' faults?

2 Human representatives of the churches: Authorised bishops/overseers preside over each congregation. Could an individual leader be held responsible for the character of the congregation? Is there any evidence for the idea of a monarchical bishop in the first century?

3 Personifications of the churches: Spiritual counterparts of earthly congregations dwell in heaven and are subject to change according to the behaviour of their complementary entities on earth. Are the stars the heavenly counterparts? Are the lampstands the earthly congregations?

4 Human messengers: The book may have been distributed through messengers who were delegates of each community. Could human messengers be symbolised by stars? Could such human messengers represent the faults and virtues of each community?

Option 3 is probably correct. The churches themselves are privileged and responsible as the true people of God. Their earthly conduct reflects their heavenly relationship to the Sovereign of this world and the next.

What does the book say about God and Jesus?

Revelation 4 and 5 is the turning point of the book. It looks back to the messages to the churches. It looks forward to the unfolding of the judgement and salvation of God. Readers ancient and modern are reminded that heaven is near for those with eyes to see. In God's good time they are assured that the will of the Lord and the Lamb shall be done on earth as in heaven. The heavenly worship provides the perspective of faith for the sufferings of believers on earth.

God the creator is addressed as *worthy* of *glory and honour and power* for two reasons. First, God created everything. Second, everything came into existence for the sake of God's good will. *You are worthy, our Lord and God, to receive glory and honour and power, for you created all things, and by your will they existed and were created. (4:11)*

God the redeemer is Christ the victorious Lion and the dying Lamb. *You are worthy to take the scroll and to open its seals, for you were slaughtered and by your blood you ransomed for God saints from every tribe and language and people and nation; you have made them to be a kingdom and priests serving our God, and they will reign on earth. (5:9-10)* He is considered worthy because he is able to open the seals of the scroll of God's redemptive plan for the destiny of the world.

At the end of Revelation 4 and 5 God and his Son receive praise and worship. *To the one seated on the throne and to the Lamb be blessing and honour and glory and might for ever and ever! (5:13)* The Lord of creation and the Lamb of redemption share the throne at the heavenly headquarters.

What sort of God do Christians believe in?
A Modern Case Study: Antony Flew
Antony Flew was born in 1923, the son of a well known Methodist New Testament scholar, R. Newton Flew. However, by 1938 Antony had become an atheist. He could not reconcile the existence of a good and powerful God with the problem of evil. In 1950 he presented a paper entitled 'Theology and Falsification' to the Socratic Club at Oxford. Its main point was to clarify the nature of religious claims. As he put it, 'Do the numerous qualifications surrounding theological utterances result in their dying the death by a thousand qualifications?' Although he was challenging religious believers to explain how their statements could be understood in the face of conflicting data, his essay led to the writing of such books as *God and Philosophy* (1966) and *The Presumption of Atheism* (1976). Flew was an atheist for sixty years. He engaged in two very well attended public debates with Thomas Warren at Denton, Texas, in 1976 and William Lane Craig at Madison, Wisconsin, in 1998. Flew and his opponents stood their ground and defended their positions. In a public debate at New York University in 2004 he surprised the audience by announcing at the beginning that he now accepted the existence of God. A debate turned into an exploration. Flew acknowledged the importance of recent work on the origin of life which pointed to the activity of a Mind behind it all. Flew had come to believe that he had to follow the argument wherever it leads.

He identified three questions as the rationale for his discovery of the God of Aristotle, the God known by reason, the God of natural theology:

> How did the laws of nature come to be?
> How did life as a phenomenon originate from non-life?
> How did the physical universe come into existence?

Flew did not claim any personal experience of God by revelation and faith. Flew agreed with the view that the God of Judaism and Christianity is similar to the God of Aristotle: a self-existent, immutable, immaterial, omnipotent, and omniscient Being. Flew's discovery of God was a pilgrimage of reason.

In 2007 Flew with Roy Abraham Varghese published *There is a God*. At the end of his deliberations, Flew allowed that Christianity 'is the one religion that most clearly deserves to be honoured and respected whether or not its claim to be a divine revelation is true.' In terms of the biblical record, it may be said that Antony Flew came to a belief in the God of creation. He does not appear to have gone on to a belief in the God of redemption. However, his journey from atheism to theism was astonishing to believers and unbelievers alike. Flew died in 2010.

According to the New Testament, the God of the Old Testament is the creator of the universe who is revealed in Jesus the Messiah and through the Spirit of Jesus as the redeemer of the universe. He is more than the God of Aristotle, he is the God of revelation and faith. He comes into focus when we look at the person and work of Jesus.

What did John expect to happen soon?
The time is near. (Revelation 1:3; 22:10)
1 The final crisis of world history: Does John expect the return of Christ in victory and judgement? In a sequential reading it appears that the seven letters, the seven seals, the seven trumpets, the seven sights, the seven bowls, and the seven judgements lead to the seven promises, including the victory of the Lord and the Lamb. John describes events which are to begin soon and will be completed in their entirety quickly. By measuring human affairs with divine measures John sets his time in the context of the last time and interprets his situation in terms of the last time.
2 The persecution of the church: Does John expect the persecution of the followers of Jesus? It seems that the picture language of the book discloses the real suffering of witnesses to Christ. Persecuted witnesses to Jesus are mentioned throughout the book: Antipas at Pergamum, souls under the heavenly altar, rewarded saints, victorious martyrs, saints and witnesses whose blood was shed, and souls of the beheaded. John emphasises the place of such suffering in the eternal purpose of God.
3 A possible solution: Does John identify what is already happening in the persecution of Christians at different times and places? Does John's viewpoint foreshadow what is not yet happening but will happen at the end in the victory of God? Is this the reason why the Revelation to John with its theology of hope becomes so relevant in the times of crisis for suffering followers of Jesus?

Who is past, present and future in the book?

"I am the Alpha and the Omega," says the Lord God, who is and who was and who is to come, the Almighty. (Revelation 1:8)

1 *The Alpha and the Omega* are the first and last letters of the Greek alphabet. God is at the beginning and at the end (1:8). Christ shares the title of *the Alpha and the Omega* as judge of the world. Christ has divine authority to execute judgement at his coming (22:13).

2 The description of the Lord God, *who is and who was and who is to come (1:8)*, is an example of 'a grammar of Ungrammar' in Revelation. Literally, the Greek reads 'from the being and the was and the coming'. Possibly this was a set phrase among Christians for the eternity and unchangeableness of God. God was from the beginning, exists now, and continues into eternity.

3 *The Almighty* is used in the Greek Version of the Old Testament to translate two Hebrew names for God: 'LORD of Hosts' (YHWH Sebaoth) and 'God Almighty' (El Shaddai). God is in control of the universe and the course of history. The title *the Almighty* occurs seven times in the Revelation to John (1:8; 4:8; 11:17; 15:3; 16:7; 19:6; 21:22).

These three aspects lead to an important conclusion: The beginning, the middle, and the end are not unrelated events but are focussed in the one and only God. From God the world comes, through God the world exists, and to God the world goes. God the Father shares his title, purpose, and throne with Jesus the Lamb of God. They are the beginning of history and the end of history and the Lord of all that is in between.

Postscript

As I have written this book I have sought to follow the evidence wherever it leads. When I first read the Bible as a young Christian, a Sunday School teacher introduced me to an interpretation of the Revelation to John. This interpretation was indebted more to the notes of a particular Bible than to the Bible itself. Since then I have learned to read the Bible to ascertain what it meant in its own time and what it means in our time. I trust that my readers will have a better understanding of the Revelation to John after they have considered my reflections.

One very hot summer morning our urban home had its regular termite inspection by a man named John. After the inspection I asked if he knew the meaning of his name. He did not. So I told him that it came (through Greek) from Hebrew for 'The Lord has shown grace.' We said goodbye until next time. A few minutes later he returned unexpectedly and asked if I could help. Two boobook owls, too young to fly, were stranded down our street. They had been blown by the hot wind out of their nest somewhere high in the trees.

We managed to collect the birds in a box. They would not have survived either the busy road or the train track nearby in the summer heat. I said to John that he had lived out the meaning of his name by showing grace in rescuing the boobook owls. After some phone calls, I transported them to a fauna rescue house. The birds would have time to mature in an aviary before they would be released into a safe rural environment.

The Revelation to John is indeed a book that says, 'The Lord has shown grace.' It begins with a greeting, *Grace to you and peace from him who is and who was and who is to come, and from the seven spirits who are before his throne, and from Jesus Christ, the faithful witness, the firstborn of the dead, and the ruler of the kings of the earth. (Revelation 1:4-5)* It ends with a benediction, *The grace of the Lord Jesus be with all the saints. Amen.(Revelation 22:21)*

The promises and blessings of the Revelation to John continue to enable twenty-first century seekers after truth to overcome fear of death, fear of guilt and fear of meaninglessness through Christ who defeated the powers of the grave, the horrors of the devil and the emptiness of the godless.

The examples of the Martyrs of the Twentieth Century reinforce the message of the book of Revelation. Each martyr knew the truth of the statement, 'The end is not an event but a person.' In the face of injustice, persecution, religious prejudice, dictatorial rule, antichristian fanaticism, wartime brutality and revolutionary madness the ten stood tall by faith through grace. Truly, the kingdom of the world has become the kingdom of our Lord and of his Messiah.

Douglas Steere, Quaker mystic, once spoke about his habit of reading the Bible with his wife each morning. He recalled the remark of an African to a foreign missionary. "Sir, it is not I who am reading the Bible. It is the Bible that is reading me!" ' The promises and blessings of the Revelation to John are not so much being read by us as they are reading us.

>The challenge remains for us:
>*Let anyone who has an ear*
>*listen to what the Spirit is saying.*

Appendix: Outline of the Book of Revelation

1:1-8	Introduction: *Apocalypse* *Prophecy* *Epistle*
1:9-20	A Vision of Christ: *The Son of Man*
2:1-3:22	The Seven Lampstands: *Ephesus* *Smyrna* *Pergamum* *Thyatira* *Sardis* *Philadelphia* *Laodicea*
4:1-5:14	A Vision of Heaven: *The Lord and the Lamb*
6:1-17; 8:1-5	The Seven Seals: *The White Horse* *The Red Horse* *The Black Horse* *The Pale Green Horse* *The Martyrs* *A Great Earthquake* *Prayers of the Saints*
7:1-17	Interlude: *The Church Militant and Triumphant*
8:6-9:21; 11:15-19	The Seven Trumpets: *Hail, Fire, Blood* *Eruption of a Volcano* *Pollution of Water* *Darkness* *Swarms of Locusts* *War Horses* *Coming of the Kingdom*
10:1-11:14	Interlude: *Eating the Scroll* *Measuring the Temple* *Prophesying by Two Witnesses*

12:1-14:5; 14:14-15:4	The Seven Sights: *Woman, Child, Dragon* *Beast from the Sea* *Beast from the Land* *The Lamb and the Church* *The Son of Man* *Harvest of Grapes* *The Song of the Lamb*
14:6-13	Interlude: *The Three Angels*
15:5-16:21	The Seven Bowls: *Curse on the Earth* *Curse on the Sea* *Curse on the Rivers* *Curse on the Sun* *Curse on the Throne of the Beast* *Curse on the Euphrates* *Curse on the Air*
17:1-20:3	The Seven Judgements: *The Great Whore* *The Great City* *The Marriage of the Lamb* *The Word of God* *The Angel in the Sun* *The Beast's Defeat* *The Devil's Imprisonment*
20:4-22:5	The Seven Promises: *The Thousand Years* *The Judgement of Evil* *New Heaven and New Earth* *Their God and My Children* *The Holy City* *The Light of the City* *The River of Life*
22:6-21	Conclusion: *Authenticity* *Imminence*

Select Bibliography

Barclay, William. *The Daily Study Bible The Revelation of John Volumes 1-2* (Saint Andrew Press, 1976)

Bauer, Walter. *A Greek-English Lexicon of the New Testament and other Early Christian Literature* Third edition revised and edited by Frederick William Danker (University of Chicago Press, 2000)

Bauernfeind, F. 'nikao', *Theological Dictionary of the New Testament* Translated by Geoffrey W. Bromiley (Eerdmans, 1967) 4:942-945

Beasley-Murray, G. R. *The Book of Revelation* (Oliphants, 1974)

Blainey, Geoffrey. *A Short History of Christianity* (Viking, 2011)

Blass, Friedrich and Debrunner, Albert. *A Greek Grammar of the New Testament and other Early Christian Literature* Translated and edited by Robert W. Funk (University of Chicago Press, 1967)

Blevins, James L. *Revelation as Drama* (Broadman, 1984)

Boxall, Ian. *The Revelation of Saint John* (A. & C. Black, 2006)

Brown, Raymond E. *An Introduction to the New Testament* (Doubleday, 1997)

Buechner, Frederick. *Now and Then* (HarperCollins, 1983)

Caird, G. B. *The Revelation of St John the Divine* (A. & C. Black, 1966)

Chandler, Andrew. Editor. *The Terrible Alternative: Christian Martyrdom in the Twentieth Century* (Cassell, 1998)

Clark, Victoria. *Why Angels Fall: A Journey Through Orthodox Europe from Byzantium to Kosovo* (Picador, 2001)

Collins, Francis S. *The Language of God: A Scientist Presents Evidence for Belief* (Free Press, 2007)

Dawn, Marva. *Joy in Our Weakness: A Gift of Hope from the Book of Revelation* (Eerdmans, 2002)

Flew, Antony with Roy Abraham Varghese. *There is a God: How the World's Most Notorious Atheist Changed His Mind* (HarperOne, 2007)

Galli, Mark. Editor. 'The End. A History of the Second Coming', *Christian History*, Issue 61 (CTi, 1999)

Gorman, Michael J. *Reading Revelation Responsibly Uncivil Worship and Witness: Following the Lamb into the New Creation* (Cascade Books, 2011)

Grass, Tim. *F. F. Bruce: A Life* (Eerdmans, 2012)

Hauck, F. 'makarios', *Theological Dictionary of the New Testament* Translated by Geoffrey W. Bromiley (Eerdmans, 1967) 4:362-370

Hemer, Colin J. *The Letters to the Seven Churches in Their Local Setting* (Eerdmans, 2001)

Hinson, E. Glenn. *Spiritual Preparation for Christian Leadership* (Upper Room Books, 1999)

_____ *A Miracle of Grace* (Smyth & Helwys, 2012)

Hull, William E. *Verbatim A Collection of Quotes ...* (Samford University, 1996)

McLaren, Brian. *The Secret Message of Jesus: Uncovering the Truth That Could Change Everything* (W Publishing Group, 2006)

Minear, Paul S. *I Saw a New Earth* (Corpus Books, 1968)

Moltmann, Jürgen. *A Broad Place: An Autobiography* Translated by Margaret Kohl (Fortress Press, 2008)

Moule, C. F. D. *An Idiom-Book of New Testament Greek* (Cambridge, 1963)

Powell, Mark Allan. *Introducing the New Testament* (Baker Academic, 2009)

Reddish, Mitchell G. *Revelation* (Smyth & Helwys, 2001)

Robertson, A. T. *A Grammar of the Greek New Testament in the Light of Historical Research* (George H. Doran Company, 1923)

Rowland, Christopher C. 'Revelation', *The New Interpreter's Bible*, 12:501-743 (Abingdon, 1998)

Rowston, Doug. *A Bird's Eye View of the Bible Second Edition* (GRACE & PEACE BOOKS, 2022)

_____ *Pray & Sing: Prayers & Songs in the New Testament* (GRACE & PEACE BOOKS, 2022)

Schweitzer, Albert. *The Quest of the Historical Jesus* (Macmillan, 1968)

Smalley, Stephen S. *The Revelation to John: A Commentary on the Greek Text of the Apocalypse* (IVP, 2005)

St. John-Smith, Emma. Compiler. *Christian Martyrs of the Twentieth Century* (Westminster Abbey, 1998)

Steere, Douglas V. 'Spiritual Renewal in Our Time', *Union Seminary Quarterly Review*, 17:33-56 (November, 1961)

Stewart, James S. 'What the Spirit is saying to the churches', *River of Life*, pp.180-191 (Hodder & Stoughton, 1972)

Stone, Hoa Van. *Heart of Stone My Story* (Company of Grace, 2007)

Turner, Nigel. 'Revelation', *Peake's Commentary on the Bible*, pp. 1043-1061 (Nelson, 1962)

Witherington, III, Ben. *Revelation* (Cambridge, 2003)

_____ *Incandescence: Light Shed through the Word* (Eerdmans, 2006)

Wright, N. T. *Revelation for Everyone* (SPCK, 2011)

_____ *The New Testament for Everyone* (SPCK, 2011)

Zerwick, Max. *A Grammatical Analysis of the Greek New Testament Vols. 1 & 2* Translated and revised by Mary Grosvenor (Biblical Institute Press, 1974, 1979)

_____ *Biblical Greek* Translated and revised by Joseph Smith (Biblical Institute Press, 1963)

Dr Doug Rowston lives in Adelaide, South Australia, with his wife Rosalie and their noble canine a Welsh Corgi dog. He is a Baptist Minister who has worked as theological lecturer at Burleigh College, religious education teacher at Prince Alfred College, pastor of Richmond Baptist Church, and adjunct lecturer at St Barnabas College (Charles Sturt University).

Doug has also written *A Bird's Eye View of the Bible (Second Edition); Jesus and Life: Word Pictures in John's Gospel; Pray and Sing: Prayers and Songs in the New Testament; Things that Jesus said: Parables of the Kingdom & Eternal Life; Things that Jesus did: Miracles of the Kingdom & Signs of Eternal Life; From Unread to Misread: Hebrews to Revelation Neglected New Testament Books.*

www.ingramcontent.com/pod-product-compliance
Lightning Source LLC
Chambersburg PA
CBHW030301010526
44107CB00053B/1774